THE BIBLE
IN POETRY

Volume 1: The Old Testament

TERESA SCHULTZ

The Bible in Poetry
Volume One: The Old Testament
Copyright © 2017 by Teresa Schultz

Published by Clay Bridges
www.claybridgespress.com

All rights reserved. No part of the publication may be reproduced, stored in a retrieval system, or transmitted in any form by any means, electronic, mechanical, photocopy, recording, or otherwise, without the prior permission of the publisher, except as provided for by USA copyright law.

All Scripture quotations, unless otherwise indicated, are taken from the Holy Bible, New International Version®, NIV®. Copyright ©1973, 1978, 1984, 2011 by Biblica, Inc.™ Used by permission of Zondervan. All rights reserved worldwide. www.zondervan.com The "NIV" and "New International Version" are trademarks registered in the United States Patent and Trademark Office by Biblica, Inc.™

Scripture quotations marked NLT are taken from the Holy Bible, New Living Translation, copyright ©1996, 2004, 2007, 2013, 2015 by Tyndale House Foundation. Used by permission of Tyndale House Publishers, Inc., Carol Stream, Illinois 60188. All rights reserved.

ISBN 10: 1939815258
ISBN 13: 9781939815255
eISBN 10: 1939815266
eISBN 13: 9781939815262

Special Sales: Most Clay Bridges titles are available in special quantity discounts. Custom imprinting or excerpting can also be done to fit special needs. Contact Clay Bridges.

To God the Father, my Lord and Savior Jesus Christ, and His precious Holy Spirit;

I am so thankful for the gift of salvation given to me by God through His Son, the personal and intimate relationship I have with Jesus, and the inspiration of the Holy Spirit.

For my mom, thank you for showing me what a strong woman looks like. I miss you more than I can say, but I know you are happy in the arms of the Savior.

For my husband, my children, and my mother-in-love, thank you for always being there.

To Rosie and the rest of my church family at UHBC, thank you for cultivating people who make Jesus known.

For Susie, thank you for your constant wisdom, support, and encouragement, and for never giving up on me.

To all the people in my life who have spoken the truth in love to me, thank you. I would not be where I am without you. (Ephesians 4:15).

For Teddy, thanks for helping me with this book.

For Pat, thanks for introducing me to Lucid Books.

To my few and faithful readers, thank you for reading and buying my book.

I hope you enjoy it.

TABLE OF CONTENTS

INTRODUCTION 1

SECTION ONE: THE BOOKS OF LAW 5

   CHAPTER ONE: GENESIS 7
      Creation 7
      Abraham 9
      Sidebar: Abram and Lot 10
      Sidebar: Abraham and Sarah 11

   CHAPTER TWO: EXODUS 15
      Moses 15
      Sidebar: Moses 17
      The Tabernacle 18

   CHAPTER THREE: LEVITICUS 21
      The Burnt Offering 21
      Sidebar: The Offering 23

   CHAPTER FOUR: NUMBERS 25
      Joshua and Caleb 25
      Sidebar: Joshua, Caleb, and Moses 27
      Balaam 29

   CHAPTER FIVE: DEUTERONOMY 31
      A New Generation 31
      Sidebar: The Children of Israel 33

SECTION TWO: THE BOOKS OF HISTORY 35

CHAPTER SIX: JOSHUA 37
Joshua 37
Jericho 39
Sidebar: Gilgal 40

CHAPTER SEVEN: JUDGES 43
Judges 43
Gideon 45
Sidebar: Gideon's Army 46
Sampson 48

CHAPTER EIGHT: RUTH 51
Love Story 51

CHAPTER NINE: 1 SAMUEL 53
Samuel 53
Saul 55
Sidebar: Saul 57
David the Boy 59
David the Man 61
Sidebar: Abigail 63

CHAPTER TEN: 2 SAMUEL 65
David the King 65
David the Father 67
Sidebar: David 68

CHAPTER ELEVEN: 1 KINGS 73
Solomon 73
Kings of Israel 75
Elijah 76
Ahab and Jezebel 80

CHAPTER TWELVE: 2 KINGS 83
Elisha 83
Sidebar: Naaman 86
Hezekiah and the Rest of the Kings of Judah 88
Sidebar: The Tribe of Dan 90

CHAPTER THIRTEEN: 1 AND 2 CHRONICLES 95
Chronicles 95

CHAPTER FOURTEEN: EZRA 97
Ezra 97

CHAPTER FIFTEEN: NEHEMIAH 99
Nehemiah 99
Wreck My Heart 101

CHAPTER SIXTEEN: ESTHER 103
Esther 103

SECTION THREE: MAJOR PROPHETS 107

CHAPTER SEVENTEEN: ISAIAH 109
Isaiah the Prophet 109
Hope for the Future 111
God's Chosen 114
Sidebar: Isaiah 117
God Remembers 118

CHAPTER EIGHTEEN: JEREMIAH 121
Jeremiah the Prophet 121
The Fall of the Kingdom of Judah 124
I Know the Plans 128

CHAPTER NINETEEN: LAMENTATIONS 131
The Lamentations of Jeremiah 131

CHAPTER TWENTY: EZEKIEL 135
The Watchman 135
The Restoration of God's People 138
Breathe on My Dry Bones 139
Sidebar: Ezekiel 140

CHAPTER TWENTY-ONE: DANIEL 143
The Fiery Furnace 143
The Lion's Den 146

SECTION FOUR: THE MINOR PROPHETS **149**

- CHAPTER TWENTY-TWO: HOSEA 151
  - God's Faithful Love 151
- CHAPTER TWENTY-THREE: JOEL 155
  - What the Locusts Have Destroyed 155
- CHAPTER TWENTY-FOUR: AMOS 157
  - From Shepherd to Prophet 157
  - Sidebar: Amos 159
- CHAPTER TWENTY-FIVE: OBADIAH 161
  - A Fire and a Flame 161
- CHAPTER TWENTY-SIX: JONAH 163
  - A Fish Called Grace 163
  - Sidebar: Jonah 165
- CHAPTER TWENTY-SEVEN: MICAH 169
  - What God Requires 169
- CHAPTER TWENTY-EIGHT: NAHUM 171
  - Nineveh Again 171
- CHAPTER TWENTY-NINE: HABAKKUK 173
  - The Lord's Justice 173
  - Sidebar: Habakkuk 174
- CHAPTER THIRTY: ZEPHANIAH 177
  - I the Lord, Have Spoken 177
- CHAPTER THIRTY-ONE: HAGGAI 181
  - Rebuilding God's House 181
- CHAPTER THIRTY-TWO: ZECHARIAH 183
  - Return to Me 183
- CHAPTER THIRTY-THREE: MALACHI 187
  - Dishonoring the Lord 187

Addiction is a force of nature. Like a tornado, it can carry you up high and drop you down hard. Sometimes beyond human control, it carries you from the edge of reality to the depths of despair and insanity. Just like a storm, the results can be catastrophic and devastating, and like a flood, you keep climbing—waiting to be rescued! But sometimes, rescue does not come when or how you think it should. Then you must decide whether to sink or swim. And just like the aftermath of a storm, some things can be salvaged and some things are gone forever. And sometimes, your whole life burns down around you. Just know that God can make beauty from ashes.

For those like me, who struggle, may you find rescue. Let God turn your ashes into something beautiful.

INTRODUCTION

Just as God persistently called Samuel in 1 Samuel 3:1–10 and consistently spoke to the woman at the well in John 4:7–26, God has persistently and consistently pursued me throughout my life.

When I suffered abuse as a child and when I lost my first love to cancer at the age of 19, God was there. When I rebelled and found myself spiraling out of control in a cycle of addiction and self-destructive behavior, God persistently spoke truth to me through my best friend Rhonda. And when I hit rock bottom, she sent me a plane ticket inviting me to live with her in Arkansas.

When I turned back to God and began seeking Him, a childhood crush from Texas that I had not seen in years suddenly moved to Arkansas. We were married several months later. That was 28 years ago. We are still married and blessed with two amazing children. God's will was constant in my life. Even though I rebelled, disobeyed, fell, and ran away more times than I can count, each time the God of Second Chances pursued me!

In Exodus 28:1–3 and Exodus 32:1–5, Aaron was called to the position of high priest. A short time later, he led the Israelites in a rebellion and made them an idol to worship. God gave Aaron a second chance, allowing him to serve as Israel's first priest.

Each time I fell from grace, I had the potential to take others down with me, and sometimes I did. And each time, I thought I could not be redeemed. But God always forgave me, and He always brought something good out of the turmoil.

Through journaling during my stay in rehabilitation, I began to enjoy writing. Then God gave me the desire to study His Word, to be transparent, and to help others through my writing. This was my second chance.

Jesus's disciple Peter walked on water. He was called by Jesus. Yet he denied Christ not just once, but three times. Still God used Peter to build the Church. He called Peter to preach His Gospel.

When I rebelled and ran from God again, He once again pursued me with relentless persistence. This time He used my godly friend Susie to seek me out and bring me back. And when it was time for me to begin a different type of ministry, God persistently sent signs so that when my friend Rosie began gently nudging me, I knew God was calling me to something new. God has given me another chance. He is using the pain, abuse, sins, and addiction of my past to show others that He is the God of second chances and that He can use anyone or anything.

Luke 15:1–32 tells three stories about the human spirit's ability to rejoice after facing adversity. In the first story, a sheep wanders off and gets lost; the shepherd leaves his flock to find and bring the sheep back. In the second, a woman loses a priceless coin. She searches everywhere, leaves no stone unturned, and does not stop until she finds the priceless coin.

The third story recounts the tale of the prodigal son who turns his back on his father, squanders his inheritance, and falls into a pit of despair. He doesn't know what else to do but go home and hope his father will forgive him. The father sees him down the road, runs to him, hugs him, and throws a party because his son has returned home safe.

Like these three stories each time I foolishly wandered off, got lost, or deliberately turned my back on God, He relentlessly pursued me, brought me home, welcomed me back, and threw a party for me in Heaven.

> *There will be more rejoicing in Heaven over one sinner who repents than over ninety-nine righteous persons who do not need to repent.*
>
> *Luke 15:7*

> *There is rejoicing in the presence of the angels of God over one sinner who repents.*
>
> *Luke 15:10*

INTRODUCTION

We serve the God of second chances who loves us with unconditional, everlasting, relentless, faithful, and gracious love. When we are lost, He saves us. When we have wandered far from home, He salvages the destruction of our rebellion into something beautiful and useful for Him. There has never been a time that God has not had His hand on our lives. He has consistently and persistently pursued us—even when we did not seek Him.

Jesus came to bring life more abundantly. He came to save the soul-sick, to deliver those bound up in sin, to break the chains of bondage and addiction. He came to heal the hurting, and comfort and restore the used, abused, bruised, battered, and broken. He came to forgive the worst sinner and to bring life to the lifeless. He came to reconcile us with God so we can have relationship with our Father. He came for us. He suffered for us. He bled for us. He died for us. He has a plan for us. He can and will use us. No matter how inadequate, insufficient, or unworthy we may feel, if God calls us, He will equip us. We never have to do anything alone. God's presence always goes with us.

SECTION ONE

The Books of Law

CHAPTER ONE

GENESIS

She gave this name to the Lord who spoke to her: "You are the God who sees me," for she said, "I have now seen the One who sees me."

Genesis 16:13

CREATION

(Genesis Chapters 1–10)

God created the entire universe from naught,
then light, dark, night, and day were wrought.
On day two, God separated the water and the sea,
then created land, plants, and trees on day three.

Day four He made the sun, the moon, and the stars in the sky.
On day five, He created creatures that swim and birds that fly.
Then He created wild animals on day six, and,
in His own image, He created man.

But God did not want Adam to be alone,
so He created Eve from Adam's rib bone.
On the seventh day, God took a break
from all the beauty He had made.

He placed mankind in the garden to live and thrive,
but the serpent tempted Eve, and she believed a lie.
They were disobedient, and mankind fell.
But that's not the end; there is more to tell.

Adam and Eve were banished from Eden,
but God promised the serpent would be beaten.
Adam and Eve were fruitful and multiplied.
Cain committed the first murder, and Abel died.

Many years later, a man named Noah was born.
But the world became evil, and God began to mourn.
He was sad that He ever created mankind,
but Noah was righteous and God called him "Mine."

So Noah built an ark to save him and his household,
along with every kind of animal—twofold.
Then God's hand shut the door,
as the waters began to rain and pour.

The rains came for forty days and nights,
until there was no more land in sight.
And when the water finally abated,
the dove never returned after Noah waited.

So Noah and his family all left the ark,
as all the animals began to disembark.
God promised never again to flood the earth,
and with a rainbow, came the promise of new birth.

ABRAHAM

(Genesis Chapters 11–50)

Abram, a descendant of Noah, took his family.
He left their home and went willingly.
God promised Abram he would be the father of a great nation.
So Abram worshipped God and built an altar of dedication.

Abram and his nephew Lot soon parted ways.
Lot chose Sodom and Gomorrah, while Abram stayed.
Lot thought the grass was greener on the other side
because of his discontent, ungratefulness, and pride.

The cities were terrible, evil, and full of crime.
God warned Abram that He would destroy them in time.
Abram rescued Lot while the cities were under attack,
and Lot's wife turned to salt when she looked back.

Abram and Sarai grew impatient with God's plans.
They took matters into their own hands.
Abram had a baby with their servant Hagar,
then Sarai's jealousy sent Hagar afar.

Abram became Abraham and Sarai become Sarah.
Sarah had a son, and she was no longer barren.
In their old age Isaac was born—
the promise of God to them sworn.

God asked Abraham for a sacrifice.
Abraham, in faith, was obedient to oblige.
He offered his only son as a sacrificial lamb,
but in his place, God sent a ram.

Isaac married Rebekah and had two boys.
Jacob stole Esau's birthright in an evil ploy.
Jacob and Esau went their separate ways,
then they reconciled after many days.

Jacob fell in love with beautiful Rachel,
the youngest daughter of Laban, his uncle.
He worked hard for seven years, so they could wed.
But Laban tricked him, and he married Leah instead.

So Jacob worked another seven years.
For Rachel, he gave blood, sweat, and tears.
Leah gave birth to many sons,
and finally, Rachel bore his favorite one.

Joseph was the youngest son with his many-colored coat.
But his brothers were jealous as their father would dote.
So they plotted to kill their own sibling,
but instead sold him into a slave ring.

As Jacob mourned believing his son was dead,
Joseph was taken to Egypt to serve their head.
Working for Pharaoh, Joseph was in high demand,
After interpreting dreams, he became second in command.

Joseph was reunited with his family.
His brothers were terrified at the reality.
They expected retaliation, but instead Joseph understood,
and said, "I forgive you. God worked it out for good!"

Sidebar: Abram and Lot

IS THE GRASS REALLY GREENER?

When Lot was given his choice of land, he chose the lusher, greener pastures close to the sinful cities of Sodom and Gomorrah. He lost his wife and was nearly destroyed because of his choice to participate in the sinful actions of those cities.

Life is vastly different when we are content in the knowledge and service of God versus when we are constantly searching for something better or the "greener grass" on the other side.

Each time we reject God, ignore His rebuke, or rebel when we don't get our way, we inevitably end up eating the bitter fruit of living our way and choking on our schemes. Every time I let myself be lulled into complacency, I find myself being held captive by sin. Yet God loves me so much that He rescues me—sometimes using my personal "Abraham" to bring me back.

Being content to walk with God brings peace in the midst of uncertainty. It brings wisdom in the unknown. It brings contentment in any situation and grace in every circumstance. It brings mercy and forgiveness in sin and blessed assurance in condemnation. It brings freedom from captivity. Walking with God brings light and air into the pit, as God reaches down to rescue us when we fall. It leads to greener pastures that are not found anywhere else.

Sidebar: Abraham and Sarah

THE GOD WHO SEES

In the story of Abraham and Sarah, they doubted God's promise and took matters into their own hands. Sarah was worried that God would take too long and that they would be too old to have a child, so she told Abraham to sleep with her servant Hagar. But then trouble arose between the two women, and Hagar ran away. While Hagar was hiding out in the wilderness, God came to her and told her about the son she would have. He encouraged her. She responded by calling God by another name. She called Him El-Roi (the God who sees me).

God sees us no matter where we are or what state we are in. He sees us when we doubt His Word, or get impatient and try to do things on our own. He sees us when we bring suffering upon ourselves. He sees us when we rebel and run from Him. He sees the sin lurking in our hearts. God sees us when we don't deserve what is happening to us. He sees the seriousness and sincerity of our hearts. He sees us with understanding and compassion. He knows us.

You have searched me, Lord, and you know me.
Psalm 139:1

> *I revealed myself to those who did not ask for me; I was found by those who did not seek me.... I said, "Here am I, here am I." All day long I have held out my hands to an obstinate people, who walk in ways not good, pursuing their own imaginations... who say, "Keep away; don't come near me, for I am too scared for you!"*
> *Isaiah 65:1–2, 5*

God knows exactly what we need and nothing is impossible for Him. He is a Father that knows our situation and circumstance. He knows our wants and needs better than we know ourselves.

> *For the eyes of the Lord range throughout the earth to strengthen those whose hearts are fully committed to him.*
> *2 Chronicles 16:9*

> *Before they call I will answer; and while they are still speaking I will hear.*
> *Isaiah 65:24*

When we don't know what to say or how to pray, the Holy Spirit comes to us and helps us in our weakness. He knows our needs and, at the right time, intercedes on our behalf with sighs and groans too deep for words. And God, who searches our hearts, knows the mind of the Spirit because the Spirit intercedes before God on behalf of us in accordance with God's will. And God, who is deeply concerned about us, causes all things to work together as a plan for good for those who love God, and are called according to His plan and purpose (Rom. 8:26–28).

And our gracious God does exceedingly abundantly more than all we can ever ask or even imagine (Ephesians 3:20). He answers according to His will. If we do not get the answer we want or when we want it, it is because He knows we do not need it, that it is not for our good or His glory.

Our God is living and personal, and He sees us. He knows our past, present, and future. He knows our sins. He knows our hearts and our motives. He knows our pride and our pain. God sees our tears. He hears our cries. He knows the hurt deep down in our soul. He feels our pain. Our God is all-seeing, and if He sees everything, He sees each of us.

When I suffered abandonment and abuse as a child, God saw. When I lost someone special as a teenager, God saw. When I rebelled, turned my back and cursed God, He saw. When I spiraled out of control in a pit of self-destructive behavior, God saw. He cared. He loved. He hurt. He waited patiently with open arms. When people prayed for me to come back, God saw. He heard. He listened. When I ran back to Him, God saw. He accepted. He forgave. He forgot. When I fell and failed time and time again, God saw. He forgave. He forgot. He helped. He taught. He loved me through it all.

And like Joseph, we can know with confidence that God sees us. He hears us. He knows us and feels our pain. He loves us and He acts on our behalf.

CHAPTER TWO

EXODUS

God said to Moses, "I am who I am. This is what you are to say to the Israelites: 'I am has sent me to you.' ... 'The Lord, the God of your fathers—the God of Abraham, the God of Isaac and the God of Jacob—has sent me to you.'"
Exodus 3:14–15

MOSES

(Exodus Chapters 1–20)

Many years after Joseph died,
the Israelites grew and multiplied.
But the Egyptians were worried and afraid,
so they oppressed the Israelites and made them slaves.

Then the King of Egypt made a decree:
Kill all the baby boys; let the girls be.
But a baby boy was born named Moses.
His mother hid him right under their noses.

She put him in a basket on the water,
where he was found by Pharaoh's daughter.
She raised the child as one of her own.
His mother was hired to help in their home.

So Moses grew up as Egyptian royalty
until one day he questioned his loyalty.
He rescued an Israelite slave who was being hurt.
He killed the abuser and buried him in the dirt.

Pharaoh heard what Moses had done,
so Moses had to go on the run.
God heard the Israelites cry with concern
and appeared in a fiery bush that would not burn.

God called to Moses to lead His people.
But Moses replied, "I am too feeble."
God told Moses, "I am that I am.
I will lead you to the Promised Land."

So Moses told Pharaoh to let God's people go.
But Pharaoh refused and told Moses no.
God sent ten plagues, then Pharaoh let them leave.
When Pharaoh followed, God parted the Red Sea.

Then Moses sang a song to the Lord.
He praised God for keeping His word.
God provided manna from Heaven and quail,
and water from a rock—He never fails.

Then God took Moses up the mountain and spoke,
He gave Ten Commandments that are no joke.
These commands we all should abide by.
When we do not obey, we make God cry.

The first is to always make God number one.
Then have no idols—absolutely none!

Don't use God's name in a bad way.
And take a rest on the Sabbath day.

Honor your parents, for on you they may rely.
And don't kill, cheat, steal, or lie.
Finally, do not want other people's things.
God concluded, as thunder and lightning did ring.

Sidebar: Moses

FIT FOR SERVICE

> *God called to (Moses) from the middle of the bush, "Moses! Moses!" "Here I am!" Moses replied.*
> *(God said)*
> *"Now go, for I am sending you to Pharaoh. You must lead my people Israel out of Egypt."*
> *But Moses protested to God, "Who am I to appear before Pharaoh? Who am I to lead the people of Israel out of Egypt?" God answered, "I will be with you."*
> Exodus 3:4, 10–12 NLT

Moses felt inadequate for the task God was calling him to. He felt not only insufficient but also unworthy. He asked God, "Who am I?" In essence, he was telling God, "I am nobody." I love this note from Matthew Henry's commentary: "The more fit any person is for service, commonly the less opinion he has of himself."[1] That was true for Moses, and I find it true in many instances.

No matter how unfit I may feel to be used by God or even to lead, if God calls me to it, He will equip me for it. And like Moses, I never have to do it alone. God's presence always goes with me if I am following His will.

---

1. Matthew Henry, *Matthew Henry's Commentary on the Whole Bible: Exodus*, http://www.biblegateway.com/resources/matthew-henry/Exodus.

In the presence of God, the weak become strong, the broken become whole, the shy become confident, the worthless become worthy, the unsure become wise, and the shamed become honored.

I have found that every time I have an excuse for not doing something God has called me to do, He always has an answer. Sometimes that answer means I have to overcome a fear. Sometimes it means letting God work through my weakness. Other times, it might mean that God completely removes the obstacle. Our God, the Great I Am, is faithful. He will always do what He says with or without my help. But I would rather be in the fight—and not a spectator.

THE TABERNACLE
(Exodus Chapters 21–40)

God continued to speak to Moses from the mountain,
about justice for personal injury and compensation,
about protection of personal property and social responsibility,
and about how to treat people with respect and civility.

Don't take advantage of orphans or widows,
and help your neighbor in his woes.
Give to the needy expecting nothing in return.
Don't follow the crowd, but do discern.

Do what is right and of good report,
and always tell the truth when you're in court.
Don't take bribes or oppress foreigners.
You know how it feels when that occurs.

Just as on the seventh day, all work stops;
on the seventh year, rest from your crops.
Let the poor, the forgotten, the homeless,
and the wild animals eat and be blessed.

Take time to give thanks and celebrate
when I brought you out of your slave state.

EXODUS

Celebrate also the blessings of your harvest,
and when your crops are gathered and you are blessed.

God sent an angel to guard and lead them,
and He gave them more instruction.
Collect an offering from everyone willing to share,
and build a sanctuary for worship and prayer.

Then I will come in and dwell with you.
Make an ark representing my covenant too.
Also make a table and lamp stand
to hold seven lamps, as I command.

Make a curtain to separate the holy place
and keep the ark in this special space.
Add an altar and a courtyard,
and for the priests, sacred garb.

When the Lord finished all of these commands,
He gave Moses the law written with His own hands.
Moses took the tablets and began his descent.
Down the mountain, to the people he went.

While Moses was gone, the people grew scared,
and they begged Moses's brother Aaron
to build something before whom they could bow.
Then Aaron, the priest of God, built a golden cow.

As Moses descended the mountain with the tablets and his staff,
the people worshipped the idol—the golden calf.
He saw them eating, drinking, and engaging in revelry,
and broke the tablets when he threw them angrily.

The people built the temple as God had said,
and by His glory, they were led.
A cloud led them through by day,
and at night a fire led the way.

CHAPTER THREE

LEVITICUS

Be holy because I, the Lord your God, am holy.
Leviticus 19:2

THE BURNT OFFERING

(Leviticus Chapters 1–27)

The saga of the Israelites continued:
those chosen people that God rescued.
Then God spoke to Moses again
as he sat in the temple tent within.

He spoke about bringing the burnt offering
and the grain without yeast for rising,
the fellowship offering, and the offering for sin
for those who sinned without intent.

Do not sin by not speaking out:
of injustice seen or heard about.
Offer your guilt offering for your unintentional sin
after you realize it and confess it herein.

If you commit a sin against your neighbor
by stealing, lying, or deceitful behavior;
you must not only bring an offering for favor,
but also make recompense to your neighbor.

God continued to speak about what to eat
and what to share with the priest.
Then Aaron and his sons made their offering,
and they began their ministry.

Before Aaron went into the temple,
he lifted his hands to bless the people.
In the temple tent of meeting,
God presence was beaming.

Then as Aaron came out to the crowd,
God's glory made the people bow.
Various other regulations from God were told:
circumcision, cleansing from diseases, and treating mold.

God prepared Aaron to enter the space
known as the most holy place.
God prepared him for the Day of Atonement,
when he would make sacrifice for all of their sin.

God continued with rules for priests,
Sabbath Year, Year of Jubilee,
unacceptable sacrifice, punishment for sin,
and appointed festivals to attend.

God continued with rewards for obedience
and punishment for disobedience,
 finally redeeming what is the Lord's.
"Be holy, because I am holy" were His words.

Sidebar: The Offering

WITHOUT DEFECT

The first few chapters of Leviticus talk about sacrificing to God. Over and over again, it says to bring a lamb or goat "without defect." "Without defect" is consistently mentioned throughout Leviticus. It would have been easy for the Israelites to keep the best for themselves and give God what they might not want or use. But sacrifice is the act of giving up something valued for the sake of something else regarded as more important or worthy. It's not sacrifice if it doesn't cost something. It cost God everything to see His Son broken, battered, beaten, and murdered for our sins.

It would be easy to bring God the leftovers or the things in our lives that we would miss less, but God doesn't want our leftovers. He wants the first fruits of our time, our money, our talents, and our hearts. All we are and everything we have is because of His sacrifice: we should be willing to give everything back to Him.

I have been guilty of giving God my leftovers, my second best. I give Him what's left of my time and my money. I give Him only part of my life, my heart, my trust, and my family. God cannot truly use or bless me until I give Him my all.

CHAPTER FOUR

NUMBERS

The Lord bless you and keep you; the Lord make his face shine on you and be gracious to you; the Lord turn his face toward you and give you peace.

Numbers 6:24–26

JOSHUA AND CALEB

(Numbers Chapters 1–21)

The first census of Israel was taken
counting over six hundred thousand men.
The Levites were placed in charge of the Tabernacle,
since, as Aaron's sons, the priests kept the chapel.

God commanded them about keeping the camp pure,
restitution for wrongs, and unfaithful spouses for sure.
He gave instructions about the Nazirite vow
since they were consecrated to God now.

God told Moses and his sons to bless the people.
Moses said, "May the Lord keep you peaceful.
May He bless you, and be gracious to you.
May He turn His face and shine on you."

Then the people brought gifts for the dedication
of the temple made for God's adulation.
God commanded them to celebrate Passover,
when they left Egypt after the death angel flew over.

Moses had the people make two silver trumpets
to call the people as God commanded it.
This was to call the community together,
and have the camps set out whenever.

As they traveled through the desert plain,
the people began to grumble and complain.
They took for granted God's loving care,
so He set the edge of the camp on fire.

Again the people complained that they were tired
of the manna God provided, and they desired
to return to Egypt, the land of their bondage.
For meat and vegetables, they were held hostage.

Then God provided quail for an entire month
until they were sick of it—done.
A plague struck and some of them died.
Still they traveled on with Moses as their guide.

They camped in the desert of Haran,
And sent spies to explore Canaan.
It was a land lush and lovely
flowing with milk and honey.

Ten of the spies gave negative reports:
"There are giants in the land and we fall short!"

But Joshua and Caleb believed the Lord.
They knew the power of His holy word.

Again the people began to complain,
but Joshua and Caleb soon explained,
"God will give us the land He promised.
Do not rebel, but in God, please trust."

Still, the people would not listen,
and God was upset once again.
But Moses interceded for them,
and again, God answered him.

He faithfully forgave the people anew,
but there were consequences too.
Only the faithful, the ones who had faith,
Joshua and Caleb, could enter the new place.

Sidebar: Joshua, Caleb, and Moses

WHICH ONE ARE YOU?

Oh, those ungrateful, grumbling, children of Israel! God rescued them from a life of slavery and abuse. Then at the first sign of trouble or discomfort, they were ready to run back to what they knew. They preferred the comfort of their captivity rather than their freedom following God to their Promised Land flowing with milk and honey. They became complacent and took for granted the manna that fell from Heaven every day to feed them. They had the presence of God right there with them—a cloud by day and a fire by night—leading them. Yet they wanted more.

As they approached the Promised Land, everyone wanted to turn back because they were afraid. But Joshua and Caleb didn't just believe in God. They believed God! They didn't see giants. They didn't see the impossible. They saw what God had promised. They saw that with God all things were possible.

Then there was Moses, the reluctant leader. He answered God's call and stepped up to lead even when he felt inferior, incapable, and unworthy. Even when the people he led out of Egypt by God's mighty hand began to grumble and plot against him, he interceded to God on their behalf.

> *For You said, 'The LORD is slow to anger and filled with unfailing love, forgiving every kind of sin and rebellion. But he does not excuse the guilty'.... In keeping with your magnificent, unfailing love, please pardon the sins of this people, just as you have forgiven them ever since they left Egypt.*
>
> Numbers 14:18–19 NLT

Although the grumblers never made it to the Promised Land, God forgave them.

There are three kinds of people in this story. First, there are the children of Israel. Sadly, this is the type of person I have been for most of my life. I have been nothing but an ungrateful brat who whines and complains when things don't go my way. I forget all about the goodness and faithfulness of God, and when I don't get what I want when I want it—I rebel! Not only do I keep myself from entering my Promised Land—the place God has prepared for me to live in His will—but also like the Israelites, I inevitably end up in captivity, bound up in sin and addiction, roaming around my wilderness in the same self-destructive cycle of sin and guilt.

Next, we have the faithful—Joshua and Caleb. I can see God working in me more and more, making me that person who trusts God. I am believing God more for my Promised Land. I am becoming an encourager to others. I am finding the good in situations and looking at how God will work things out. My old self reacted with self-pity and anger at bad circumstances. But God is changing me to someone who is faithful to His Word and faithful in hope.

Finally, there is Moses. He is a leader and an intercessor. He strives to obey God and lead the people in God's will. He intercedes on their behalf before God. This is who I want to be. I want to lead people to the cross. I want to approach the Throne of Grace on behalf of the lost and hurting. I want to be the person that points people to the cross and intercedes for my brothers and sisters.

Of the three kinds of people in this story, which one are you?

BALAAM

(Numbers Chapters 22–36)

Again the people whined and complained;
then many venomous snakes came.
They bit the people, and made them sick.
Moses made a bronze snake on a stick.

The people looked at the snake and lived.
God healed them when they believed.
The people continued to move ahead,
God gave them victory everywhere He led.

The King of Moab heard this and was afraid.
He called Balaam the prophet for aid.
He asked Balaam to curse the Israelites,
but God told Balaam, "These people are Mine."

Balaam told King Balak, "God said no."
King Balak summoned Balaam though.
Balaam's donkey would not stay on the road
because he could see the angel of the Lord.

Balaam was angry and began to beat the donkey.
God opened the animal's mouth, and he began to speak.
"What have I ever done to you?"
Then Balaam's eyes were opened too.

Balaam could see the angel, and the angel said,
"Go to Balak, but speak what I tell you instead."
So Balaam blessed the Israelites in front of Balak.
Balak said, "Why have you done this behind my back?"

Balaam replied, "I can only say what God puts in my mouth."
Then Balak was angry and said, "Just go home now!"
Balaam answered, "I could not do anything of my own accord,
good or bad, beyond the command of the Lord."

Then Balaam warned Balak of what would happen:
that a great king would emerge and then,
Moab will be conquered and crushed,
and the enemies of God will be dust.

As the Israelites traveled, they were seduced again.
They rebelled and were punished for their sin.
Another census was taken after deaths and births.
Then Joshua replaced Moses and led them forth.

CHAPTER FIVE

DEUTERONOMY

The Lord our God, the Lord is one. Love the Lord your God with all your heart and with all your soul and with all your strength. These commandments that I give you today are to be on your hearts. Impress them on your children. Talk about them when you sit at home and when you walk along the road, when you lie down and when you get up.

Deuteronomy 6:4–7

A NEW GENERATION

(Deuteronomy Chapters 1–34)

Those who doubted and rebelled against the Lord,
wandered in the wilderness, not moving forward.
Because of their ungratefulness and fears,
they wandered around for forty years.

Now all the people who doubted God were dead,
so it was time for the rest to move ahead.

God commanded Moses once again:
"Leave here. Go ahead to Canaan."

Moses spoke to the new generation
the words of God to His nation.
You have a God who is near you always.
Observe His commands, show wisdom all your days.

Remember all the things you have seen and learned.
Teach them to your children, and theirs in turn.
Stay away from any idol worship; serve God only.
He is the one true God—perfect and holy.

Then Moses further communicated,
the Ten Commandments he again mandated.
God promised to protect and bless them
if they listened to and obeyed Him.

The children of Israel wandered forty years about,
yet their clothes and shoes never wore out.
They always had water and food,
but they never showed any gratitude.

They wandered until they were all dead,
and only the next generation was left.
Now God was bringing them into a good land
that was promised to the descendants of Abraham.

Moses told them about food (both clean and unclean),
tithes, observing Passover, festival routines,
legal matters, going to war, and various laws,
disputes, trials, and punishment without cause.

Do not add to or take away from God's commands.
Build an altar to God in the Promised Land.
Receive blessings for obedience, curses for disobedience.
God will raise a prophet, His Word to dispense.

God renewed His covenant once again,
setting a choice before His children,
"I have set before you life and death.
Now choose life, for it is best."

Moses was one hundred and twenty years old
as he turned leadership over to Joshua, the bold.
"Be strong and courageous," Moses replied,
"God goes before you," then Moses died.

Sidebar: The Children of Israel

SECURITY

Security is one of our basic human needs. We all need to feel secure. So, why do so many of us feel more secure when we are in bondage?

We have complete security and safety in Christ, yet when times get tough, we long to be back in our prisons where we think we have everything we need and want. Our prisons make us feel safe.

For me, the four walls of my prison provided a place of no responsibility, no worries, and no problems—just as long as I got my next fix. The reality is that my prison was my death chamber. All the responsibilities, problems, and worries were still there. I just didn't care. The end result was more and bigger problems!

Three things that send me back to my prison faster than you can blink are ungratefulness, self-pity, and complaining. If I want to stay in the security of God's grace and provision, then I have to stay thankful in my security.

If I am unsure about my circumstances (whether financial, physical, or otherwise) I can choose to complain, feel sorry for myself, or be ungrateful or I can choose to be secure in God's constant provision. I can choose to be secure in my salvation and in God's love for me. I can be secure knowing that no matter what happens to my earthly possessions, I have a heavenly home. I can be secure knowing that my earthly body will be sick and fade away, but my soul will live eternally with Jesus Christ. I can be secure in the fact that God is God. He is never changing and never failing! That is a lot of security! I will be thankful in my security!

SECTION TWO

The Books of History

CHAPTER SIX

JOSHUA

But if serving the Lord seems undesirable to you, then choose for yourselves this day whom you will serve.... But as for me and my household, we will serve the Lord.

Joshua 24:15

JOSHUA

(Joshua Chapters 1–5:12)

After the death of Moses, Joshua began to lead.
"Be strong and courageous," God said. "Obey me."
So Joshua sent spies and told them to go
check out the land, especially Jericho.

While they were in Jericho, they had to hide
in the house of Rahab who was on their side.
She was a prostitute who lived in the city.
They promised to save her and her family.

They told her to tie a scarlet rope to her window,
so that when they attacked the city they would know
that she had helped the spies escape,
and capture she had helped them evade.

The Israelites camped out beside the Jordan River.
Joshua said, "Follow the Ark of the Covenant, but touch it never."
"Stand in the river when you reach the edge of the water,"
Joshua told the priests as they prepared to cross the river.

The Israelites broke camp as they began their passage.
The Jordan River was high at flood stage,
When the priest's feet touched the water of the Jordan,
the water stopped, the river no longer poured in.

After the people walked across on dry land,
They made a memorial to God's mighty hand.
About forty thousand armed men crossed the shore
to the plains of Jericho preparing for war.

They camped at Gilgal, the eastern border of Jericho.
The surrounding kings heard what God had done, so
they were afraid and no longer had courage.
Their hearts melted in fear at the knowledge.

Since all the men of military age had died in the wilderness,
The next generation was circumcised to show devoutness.
While they camped at Gilgal afterward,
they celebrated the Passover of the Lord.

The next day they ate produce of the land:
unleavened bread and roasted grain.
No longer did they eat manna from Heaven.
That year they ate the produce of Canaan.

JERICHO

(Joshua Chapters 5:13–24)

The commander of the army of the Lord
appeared to Joshua with this word:
"Take off your sandals, you're on holy ground.
God will deliver Jericho; the walls will come down.

"March around the city one time for six days.
Then have the priests carry trumpets to play.
On the seventh day, march seven times about.
After the trumpets sound, have the army give a shout.

"Then the walls of the city will fall down,
and the army will go into the town.
Then Jericho will be defeated,
and victory will be completed."

So the Israelites did as God commanded,
and that day victory was granted.
Rahab was saved along with her family.
For her faithfulness, she avoided catastrophe.

God was with Joshua, with His mighty hand,
and Joshua's fame was known throughout the land.
Once again the Israelites were unfaithful.
A man named Achan was disgraceful.

He took some things that were forbidden,
and then there were consequences given.
The Israelites conquered the city of Ai.
God renewed his covenant to abide by.

Joshua built an altar for burnt offerings,
then read aloud the curses and blessings.
The Gibeonites tricked them into a treaty.
They heard what God had done and were uneasy.

The five kings of the Amorites attacked Gibeon's city.
God made the sun and moon stand still, and then He
helped the Israelites to defeat their enemies,
along with the entire region, with ease.

There was peace in the land for a long time.
Then as Joshua grew past his prime,
God told him there were more lands to be taken
as the inheritance He promised to His nation.

The land was allotted to the Israelites.
Joshua blessed Caleb for doing right,
for being brave, faithful, and fearless
as he spied out Canaan with success.

Joshua grew into a very old man.
He began his farewell address, and
as he spoke, he reminded them of
God's commands and of His love.

Joshua reminded them to serve God only.
He said, "As for my family and me,
we will serve the Lord."
Then the people gave their word.

Joshua warned them that disaster would occur
if their disobedience and idolatry did recur.
God's covenant with them was renewed again.
Joshua died and was buried in the Promised Land.

Sidebar: Gilgal

REMOVING YOUR REPROACH

> *The Israelites had moved about in the wilderness forty years... Then the Lord said to Joshua, "Today I have rolled away the reproach of Egypt from you." So the place has been called Gilgal to this day.*
>
> *Joshua 5:6, 9*

The Israelites wandered forty years in the wilderness. They carried around the reproach of their bondage, sin, and shame following the same cycle of defeat (slavery → deliverance → temptation → idolatry/rebellion → slavery) over and over again.

Eventually the Israelites began to believe and obey God. Then they began to follow the cycle of victory (slavery → deliverance→ temptation → faith in God/faithfulness to God). Rather than continue the same cycle of defeat, the Israelites came full circle following the victory cycle and the upward spiral that led to Gilgal and their Promised Land.

I have been stuck in that spiral of defeat many times. The more I study God's word, the more I think about my testimony and how God has been calling me to step out and share with others. Now I am beginning to see my testimony in a different light, and I am overwhelmed with the desire to share it. I want to tell the world what God has done for me. I want everyone to know how God has delivered me from my cycle of defeat. I no longer feel condemnation and shame when I am reminded of my past; instead, I feel joy that God has been with me all along. I let God roll away the reproach of my sin and shame. I have reached my Gilgal.

It did not happen overnight. It was a process of continued belief and obedience in God—taking baby steps, then bigger and bigger steps until I was ready to jump into God's will with both feet. It was a process of changing my attitude and changing how I responded to situations. Rather than reacting to my circumstances with rebellion, self-pity, and self-destructive behavior, I respond to God and let Him lead me upward rather than in circles. I am overjoyed by God's faithfulness. I am ready to continue the upward spiral to the place God is calling me.

CHAPTER SEVEN

JUDGES

(The Israelites) were in great distress. Then the Lord raised up judges, who saved them…

Judges 2:15–16

JUDGES

(Judges Chapters 1–5)

The Israelites attacked and defeated Jerusalem and Hebron,
Debir, Zephath, Gaza, Ashkelon, and Ekron.
Some of the people, they did not drive out completely
but instead forced them into slavery.

The angel of the Lord came to them,
He asked why they had disobeyed Him.
"I delivered you and made my covenant too,
but your disobedience will be a snare to you."

Although the people wept aloud at His words,
the next generation grew up and forgot about the Lord.
Then the Israelites did evil in God's sight.
They worshipped idols, not doing what was right.

They forsook the Lord, God of their ancestors,
who delivered them from their oppressors.
So God's hand was no longer with the people.
They were defeated and oppressed by evil.

Then the Lord began to raise up judges,
to save the people from the enemy's clutches.
The people still would not listen
they showed no signs of contrition.

Once again they were sold into slavery,
so they cried out to God in their misery.
They continued this cycle again and again
as God called judges to help and guide them.

Othniel judged them, and they went to war.
The land had peace for forty years more.
Then after eighteen years of bondage,
God sent Ehud to be their judge.

The next judge who rescued them
was Deborah—she was a woman.
The people were oppressed for twenty years.
God heard them through their tears.

Deborah was a prophet who led the Israelites.
She encouraged Barak to win the fight.
They won the fight and sang to the Lord,
and the land had peace for forty years more.

GIDEON

(Judges Chapters 6–12)

Then, again the people did evil in God's sight.
For seven years, they were oppressed by the Midianites.
The Midianites ravaged their crops and beasts
till the Israelites were poor and had little to eat.

Then the angel of the Lord spoke to Gideon.
"God is with you, mighty warrior," he began.
But Gideon replied, "Then why did He let this happen?"
The angel replied, "God will lead you to deliver them."

Gideon said, "I am weak, and from a weak family too."
The Lord said, "Go in the strength that God gives you.
I will strike down the Midianites leaving none alive."
Then Gideon said, "If it's really You, then give me a sign."

Gideon prepared an offering for the Lord.
Then fire consumed it and left it charred.
Gideon built an altar to worship the Lord.
Then he tore down the altar of Baal—it was no more.

Gideon asked God for another sign to prove the truth.
So God made the ground dry but his fleece full of dew.
Gideon said, "Don't be angry, God; give me one more sign."
This time the ground was wet and the fleece completely dry.

Gideon started out but God said, "You have too many men."
So twenty-two thousand left in fear; there remained ten.
Then God dwindled the men down to three hundred,
so the glory would be God's for the battle ahead.

With three hundred men, the Midianites were defeated.
Then the Israelites asked Gideon to be their leader.
Gideon said, "I will not rule you. God will rule you."
Then another forty years of peace ensued.

Gideon later died at a ripe old age.
Once again, in idolatry, the people engaged.
They forgot the God that rescued them
and showed no loyalty to the family of Gideon.

Abimelek, (Gideon's son), murdered all of his brothers,
so he could be the king—and no other.
But Jotham (the youngest brother) was able to flee,
and he cursed the people for their conspiracy.

Abimelek brought death and destruction wherever he led
but was killed after a stone dropped on his head.
A man named Tola judged for twenty-three years;
then for twenty-two years, they were led by Jair.

The Israelites rebelled again and worshipped idols.
They continued in their same self-destructive cycles.
They were sold to the Philistines and the Ammonites.
They were crushed and shattered under their might.

Then, again they cried out to Him,
"Against You, God, we have sinned."
"I have rescued you again and again," God said.
But He loved them and had pity on them instead.

Jephthah led Israel for six years, and then he died.
After him, Ibzan of Bethlehem, then Elon the Zebulunite.
After him, Abdon (son of Hillel) led them.
Again the Israelites were evil and sinned.

Sidebar: Gideon's Army

WEAKNESS

In Judges, Gideon's outnumbered army defeated the enemy with each soldier using nothing but a torch, a trumpet, and a water pitcher. Winning a battle is all about using the right weapons. When we are in a spiritual battle, some of the weapons we use are our physical strength, our talents and abilities, our mind, our money, and our reputation. Often in the past, I have used lying (to myself, to God, or to others) or sarcasm to try to fight my battles. I have even retreated from the fight escaping into my addiction.

The spiritual weapons that God has given us to use are His Holy Spirit, prayer, His Word, faith, humility, worship, truth, praise, accountability, contentment, and counsel from godly friends. When I am facing spiritual warfare manifested as problems with my family, my job or my finances, I usually try to rely on my strengths, my human reasoning, my reputation, or my wealth (or lack thereof) to handle things.

More effective weapons that I should be using are patience, peace, faith, praise, prayer, and God's Word. Dealing with spiritual warfare using natural weapons will never solve the problem. We cannot win on our own. If we use the spiritual weapons God has given us (no matter how unusual we think they are), we will learn, grow, sometimes help others, and we will win.

Gideon started out with over thirty thousand men armed for battle. God told him, "You have too many men" (Judges 7:2). God needed them to know that victory came from Him and not from their power, so the glory would go to Him.

God told Gideon that all those who were afraid could leave. Twenty-two thousand men left. Then God said, "There are still too many men. Take them down to the water, and I will thin them out for you there" (Judges 7:4).

Three hundred men drank the water from cupped hands rather than kneeling down to drink the water. God told Gideon, "With the three hundred… I will save you and give the Midianites into your hands. Let all the others go home" (Judges 7:7).

On the day of the battle, Gideon did as the Lord had commanded. He divided the three hundred men into three companies giving each man a trumpet and water pitcher with a torch inside. Upon Gideon's signal, the three hundred men blew their trumpets and smashed their jars. Then they shouted, "A sword for the Lord and for Gideon" (Judges 7:20)!

The Midianites were afraid and confused. Some of them ran and some of them attacked their fellow soldiers. The Israelites defeated the vast Midianite army with a fraction of the men but with all the power of God.

Like the pitchers that held the torches, our bodies are weak and fragile, yet they hold the fire of the Holy Spirit. That fire burns in us waiting to be released so that others can see it. The light was released when the pitchers were broken. Sometimes we need to be broken to release the light in us. Our weakness allows the light of God to be seen.

There are so many things that I struggle with, but my biggest weakness is my struggle with addiction. Yet God uses my weakness to teach me, to help me grow, and to give me hope. He also uses my weakness to help others. We are fragile, frail, and fallible, yet we have been entrusted by God to carry the message of salvation. God's power dwells inside our earthen vessel. He uses us not in spite of who we are, but because of who we are and who He is making us to be.

> *(Jesus) said to me, 'My grace is sufficient for you, for my power is made perfect in weakness.' Therefore I will boast all the more gladly about my weaknesses, so that Christ's power may rest on me. That is why, for Christ's sake, I delight in weaknesses, in insults, in hardships, in persecutions, in difficulties. For when I am weak, then I am strong.*
>
> 2 Corinthians 12:9–11

SAMPSON

(And the Conclusion of Judges)
(Judges Chapters 13–21)

The people were again delivered into the hands of the Philistines.
Then came Samson, a Nazarite, whose birth was foreseen.
He grew in the Lord and was blessed and stirred.
He found a Philistine woman, and he married her.

He held a feast and told the men a riddle,
but then the men put his wife in the middle.
They threatened her and her family,
so she revealed the answer, understandably.

So they solved the riddle, and Sampson had to pay,
but he knew how they had gotten the answer right away.
And then just to add insult to injury,
Samson's wife was given to someone else from the party.

He was furious and wanted to harm them as his anger flared.
He tied together the tails of three hundred foxes in pairs.
He attached a torch to the tail of each fox;
then sent them running through their crops.

The Philistines came and tried to take him to their home,
but he slaughtered a thousand men with a donkey's jawbone.
He praised God and his strength was renewed.
He led Israel for a twenty-year interlude.

Then Sampson fell in love with Delilah (a Philistine),
but her love was not completely genuine.
She conspired to find out the secret of his strength.
In exchange for silver, she questioned him at length.

He kept tricking her by telling her lies;
then she became upset and asked him, "Why
don't you love me enough to tell me?"
So he revealed the truth to her finally.

He told her, "No razor has ever been used on my head."
So she lulled him to sleep, called the Philistines, and said,
"Come quickly, cut off his hair and his strength will leave him."
So they shaved off the braids of his hair, and he began to weaken.

Then they captured Sampson and gouged out his eyes.
The people began to mock, make fun of him, and criticize.

Then Sampson asked God to give him strength once more.
He pushed down the pillars and the temple crashed to the floor.

Everyone inside, including Sampson, died there.
Then Sampson's family came and took great care.
They buried him in between Eshtaol and Zorah
with his father in the tomb of Manoah.

Micah made idols and installed a Levite to be his priest.
There was no king and everyone did as they pleased.
The Danites came and took Micah's idols and his holy man.
They attacked, conquered, and rebuilt Laish, and named it Dan.

The Benjamites committed heinous crimes in the land.
The Israelites were furious, so they took a stand.
They got together and united as one against the city.
After three days, the Israelites defeated them without pity.

The Benjamites seized and carried away the women as their wives.
Then they returned and rebuilt their homes to occupy.
Once again, the Israelites did what they always did:
With no king, they did whatever they saw fit.

CHAPTER EIGHT

RUTH

But Ruth replied, "Where you go I will go, and where you stay I will stay. Your people will be my people and your God my God. Where you die I will die, and there I will be buried."

Ruth 1:16–17

LOVE STORY

(Ruth Chapters 1–4)

There was a woman named Naomi whose husband and sons died.
Her two daughters-in-law, Ruth and Orpah, remained by her side.
Naomi decided to go back home to get food.
She told the women to leave with her gratitude.

Orpah chose to go her own way,
while Ruth decided she would stay.
Ruth clung to her mother-in-law and vowed not to leave.
She told her, "Your people are my people. To you I will cleave.

Your God will be my God and with you I will die."
So they traveled to Bethlehem by and by.
They arrived in Bethlehem as the barley harvest was under way.
Ruth went behind the harvesters and picked up the leftovers each day.

The owner of the field was Boaz, a relative of Naomi.
He came and greeted the harvesters and asked boldly,
"Who is that woman?" he said speaking of Ruth.
Then he let her work in the fields because of the truth.

He had heard all about Ruth's loyalty.
He prayed for God to reward her richly.
He invited her to eat lunch with him.
He told his men to let her harvest with them.

Boaz told his men to help Ruth out
by pulling out stalks to leave on the ground.
Ruth was able to provide for her family
all because of Boaz's generosity.

Boaz knew Ruth was a woman of noble character.
He gave six measures of grain to take back with her.
He then bought Naomi's property,
and he took Ruth to marry.

Boaz and Ruth had a baby boy.
He brought them both great joy.
Obed was that baby boy's name,
and David would be his grandson of fame.

CHAPTER NINE

1 SAMUEL

To obey is better than sacrifice, and to heed is better than the fat of rams.

1 Samuel 15:22

SAMUEL

(1 Samuel Chapters 1–7)

There was a woman whose name was Hannah.
She was loved by her husband Elkanah.
Hannah wanted to have a child so badly
that she prayed to the Lord weeping bitterly.

"Lord, if You will bless me with a child," she prayed,
"I will give him back to You all of his days."
The Lord answered her prayer, and she had a son.
She named him Samuel and dedicated him to the Holy One.

Hannah took Samuel to the temple while he was still young.
Then she prayed a prayer of thanksgiving with her tongue.
"My heart rejoices in the Lord," she prayed.
"There is no one holy like You, God," she said.

Eli, the priest, had wicked sons.
They had no regard for the Holy One.
They treated the Lord's offering with contempt.
In His eyes, they committed great sin.

But Samuel ministered and did good in God's eyes.
Each year Hannah would make him a robe bringing it with their sacrifice.
Eli blessed Hannah, "May the Lord replace the child you gave to the Lord."
So God gave Hannah three sons and two daughters more.

While Samuel grew up in the presence of the Lord,
Eli's sons sinned more and more.
God told Eli no more priests would come from his bloodline:
"I will raise up a faithful priest, who will do what is in my mind."

One night while Samuel was sleeping, God called to him.
Samuel answered, "Here I am," finding Eli within.
Eli said, "I didn't call you. Go back to bed."
But two more times, "Samuel, Samuel," the Lord said.

When Eli realized it was God calling the boy out,
he sent Samuel back to bed without a doubt.
Eli said, "The next time you hear the word,
say, 'Your servant is listening. Speak, Lord.'"

Samuel again heard God speaking.
Samuel answered, "Your servant is listening."
God said to him, "I am about to do something in Israel,
and it will cause all who hear it to hail."

The Lord was with Samuel as he grew,
and all of Israel from Dan to Beersheba knew
that he was a prophet of the Lord,
as God revealed himself through His Word.

The Israelites went into battle with the Ark of the Covenant.
Eli's sons went with the Ark in all of their arrogance.
The Philistines captured the Ark that day,
The army was defeated, and Eli's sons slain.

When Eli heard, he died after falling back in his chair.
He was ninety-eight and had led the people for forty years.
When the Ark was away from God's people, death and destruction came.
So after seven months, the Philistines returned the Ark in shame.

The people took the Ark to Abinadab's home,
and consecrated his son Eleazar to guard as his own.
It remained there safely for twenty years in all.
Then Samuel led the people to defeat the Philistines at Mizpah.

Samuel sacrificed offerings to the Lord,
and prayed to God on the people's accord.
The Philistines were subdued, and there was peace with the Amorites.
Samuel faithfully led the people for the rest of his life.

SAUL

(1 Samuel Chapters 8–15)

As Samuel grew older, he appointed his sons as leaders.
The firstborn was Joel, and the second was Abijah.
They were dishonest, took bribes, and perverted justice.
So the people told Samuel, "We need a King to lead us."

Samuel was upset and he prayed to the Lord.
But God said, "Go ahead and listen to their words.
They are not rejecting you. They're rejecting me.
Just as they have done repeatedly."

Samuel told the people true:
"If a king rules over you,
he will take your sons for the war,
or to plow his garden, or more.

"He will take your daughters as well
to make perfume and cook, without fail.
He will take a tenth of your grain,
and the best crops in his name.

"He will take your servants and cattle for his use.
You will become his slaves, if this is what you choose."
But the people still wanted a king to govern.
So God relented knowing they would learn.

God told Samuel to anoint a man named Saul.
He was a Benjamite, handsome and tall.
Samuel presented King Saul to the crowd.
"Long live the King!" they shouted aloud.

Saul rescued the people in the city of Jabesh.
Then he was confirmed as king and blessed.
The people had Saul; they no longer needed a prophet.
But the people were still in Samuel's debt.

Samuel gave a farewell speech, words to live by:
"Fear, serve, and obey the Lord Most High."
Then he called on God to send rain and thunder
as the people looked on in awe and wonder.

Then God brought the thunder and rain,
and Samuel prayed for the people once again.
Saul began his reign at thirty years of age.
He ruled for a forty-two-year resume.

But Saul was disobedient and did not listen,
so Samuel was upset and rebuked him.

God chose someone else to fill the part:
a man of God after His own heart.

Saul's son Jonathan was courageous and brave.
While all the Israelites were hiding in caves,
Jonathan took his armor bearer to the enemy outpost.
He believed in the power of God to the utmost.

They defeated twenty of the Philistines.
The rest of the army ran from forces unseen.
Israel was saved from the battle on that day
as the Lord God kept the enemy at bay.

Saul disobeyed God once again,
so God rejected him as king.
Saul refused to take the Lord's advice.
God said, "Obedience is better than sacrifice."

Sidebar: Saul

OBEDIENCE IS BETTER THAN SACRIFICE

> *What is more pleasing to the LORD: your burnt offerings and sacrifices or your obedience to his voice? Listen! Obedience is better than sacrifice, and submission is better than offering the fat of rams. Rebellion is as sinful as witchcraft, and stubbornness as bad as worshiping idols. So because you have rejected the command of the LORD, he has rejected you as king.*
> 1 Samuel 15:22–23 NLT

Saul's mistake was his selfishness and pride. Because he thought he knew more or better than God and because he kept things that God had said to destroy, he rebelled against what God had told him to do. He made himself his own idol, putting his wants above God's commands and even going so far as to build a monument to himself.

God rejected him as king and sought out David—a man after His own heart (1 Samuel 1:14). God rejected Saul as king, but not as a person. Saul could have turned his heart back to God and repented; instead he continued to rebel against God. His heart grew bitter as his mind was tormented. He rejected God and opened himself up to Satan. The rest of his life was filled with depression, fear, and death. The only way he found peace was when David (the one who took his place as king) played the harp for him.

God chose David for his heart (1 Samuel 16:7). God saw David's faith when he was willing to face a giant armed with nothing but a slingshot (1 Samuel 17:37). God saw how David loved the Word of the Lord (Psalm 119:47–48). God saw David's transparency and honesty. Despite David's sins, throughout the Psalms, we can see that David poured out his heart to God, we even see him complain to God a little, have a pity party, but then he would turn to God, in faith, asking God for help. Then he always took time to praise God.

David fell hard when he first lusted after another man's wife and committed adultery. When he found out she was pregnant with his child, he had her husband killed by putting him on the front line in battle.

But David always came to his senses, and once he realized his sin, he was truly repentant. He turned away from his sin and toward God. That is what God looks for. Our obedience to God shows our love for Him. David loved God. That is what God saw in him.

> *The LORD detests the sacrifice of the wicked, but he delights in the prayers of the upright. The LORD detests the way of the wicked, but he loves those who pursue godliness.*
> *Proverbs 15:8–9 NLT*

I have done some bad things, been selfish, and have tried to build monuments to myself in the things I did, had, or wanted. While God may have rejected me for a specific task or area of ministry because of my sin, God never rejected me as a person. He waited for me to come to my senses, sometimes using other people (much like He used Nathan to reveal David's sin). He forgave me and gave me another chance (over and over).

To be a person after God's heart, I need to be open and receptive to His leading. I need to show my love for God through my obedience to Him. I need to show my love for Him by being faithful to praise and seek Him daily, keeping an attitude of gratitude by always finding things to be grateful for. I need to love God's Word. Finally, I need to accept God's love and forgiveness, turning away from my sin and toward Him starting every day anew just as His mercies are new every morning.

DAVID THE BOY

(1 Samuel Chapters 16–17)

As Samuel mourned for Saul, God spoke to him,
"Fill your horn with oil; find Jesse of Bethlehem.
I have chosen one of his sons to be king."
So Samuel set out, and the journey convened.

He arrived at Jesse's and saw Eliab, the oldest son,
and he thought to himself, Surely this is the one.
But God said, "I don't look at outward appearance.
I look at the heart, the will, and the spirit."

So Jesse brought out seven of his sons.
Samuel asked, "Are these the only ones?"
Jesse answered him, "There is still the youngest."
"He is watching the sheep," Jesse said in protest.

They sent for David and had him come.
He was young, healthy, and handsome.
God said, "Rise and anoint him, for he is the one."
From that day on, God's Spirit was on that son.

But God's Spirit had departed from Saul.
He was tormented by day and at nightfall.
Someone told him that David played the lyre.
Saul called for David, and the music became a pacifier.

Saul asked Jesse to let David remain in the palace.
David became an armor bearer and brought Saul solace.
Each time the evil spirit would torment the king,
David would play for the relief it would bring.

The Israelites were still at war with the Philistines.
David traveled between his home and the king.
One day Jesse sent David to the front lines
to take his three oldest brothers supplies.

A giant named Goliath came out of the Philistine camp.
Nearly ten feet tall, he was the Philistine's champ.
He defied God and terrorized the Israelite army.
He called out to them, "Who will fight me?"

He said, "If one man can beat me, we will be your slaves,
but you must serve us if the fight goes the other way."
David overheard the defiant giant and was angry.
He said, "If no one else will fight, then let me."

Saul exclaimed, "You are not able to fight this man."
David said, "I have killed lions and bears with my bare hands."
Saul tried to put his armor on David, but he could not move.
David was not used to wearing it, so he had it removed.

David went and chose five smooth stones from the stream.
He placed them in his bag and approached the Philistine.
Goliath saw David approaching with his sling, and he spit,
"Am I a dog that you come at me with sticks?"

David replied, "You come at me with a spear and sword.
But I come against you in the name of the Lord,
the Almighty God of the armies of Israel."
Then he released his sling and Goliath fell.

DAVID THE MAN

(1 Samuel Chapters 18–31)

Saul's son Jonathan was David's best friend.
They were like brothers and made a covenant.
David was a man full of ambition.
He was successful on every mission.

Soon people began singing songs about David.
Then Saul became jealous of everything he did.
From then on, Saul began to want David dead.
He even threw a spear at David's head.

Saul plotted about how he could kill the man.
He offered David his older daughter's hand
if he would just fight the battles for the king.
But she accepted another's wedding ring.

Saul's daughter Michal was in love with David,
so Saul decided to use her to bait him.
He had planned for David to fall by the hands of the enemy,
but again, David conquered them victoriously.

David continued to be victorious in battle
while Saul hated him and began to unravel.
He tried to kill David twice with his spear.
Then David had to run and hide in fear.

Saul continued to chase after David,
but Jonathan still remained his friend.
David hid in Nob with the priest of God,
then in Gath, Adullam, and Mizpah.

Saul discovered that David had hidden in Nob.
There he slaughtered the priests of God.
His man Doeg carried out his orders,
and he slaughtered the town to its borders.

David and his men continued traveling.
They saved Keilah from the Philistines.
When they heard that Saul was after them still,
they stayed in the wilderness, desert, and hills.

Twice David had the chance to kill Saul,
but David spared his life after all.
Then David gave Saul his promise
that he would not kill his descendants.

Later Samuel died and everyone mourned for him.
David moved down into the desert of Paran.
There was a wealthy man named Nabal
who had a beautiful wife named Abigail.

Nabal was mean, grouchy, and discourteous.
Abigail was intelligent and conscientious.
David sent a messenger to ask Nabal for aid.
David's men had kept Nabal's shepherds safe.

But Nabal was rude and did not care.
He was stingy, and he did not share.
One of the servants went to Abigail
and told her how David's men prevailed.

As David was on his way to Nabal, angrily,
Abigail rode out to meet David, hastily.
She loaded wine, sheep, cakes, and bread;
then she bowed low to the ground and said,

"Listen to me. I am your humble servant.
Pay no attention to my wicked husband.
Please accept these gifts with my apologies.
The Lord God will give you a lasting dynasty."

David accepted the gifts from Abigail,
and on that day, good sense prevailed.

Later, Nabal's heart failed, and he lost his life.
Then David asked Abigail to be his wife.

David continued to flee Saul
driven to hide like an outlaw.
He lived in Gath for over a year.
He had six hundred men, who were sincere.

The Amalekites raided Negev and Ziklag and burned them down.
They took all the people captive and returned to their town.
David took four hundred men and defeated them
and brought all the people back with him.

While Saul and his sons were fighting the Philistines,
the battle became fierce and extreme.
All three of Saul's sons fell in battle and died.
Then Saul fell as well, and Israel cried.

Sidebar: Abigail

SHOWING WISDOM

It is always important to make the best of every bad situation. In 1 Samuel 25:18–39, a woman named Abigail had to do exactly that. Her husband Nabal was a wicked and mean man. Even though David's men treated his people and guarded his pastures well, Nabal (rather than returning the favor) insulted and threatened David's men. This could have caused great harm to him and his family, but Abigail acted quickly. She took food and provisions to David's men.

She fell at David's feet and, begging his pardon, humbly and respectfully apologized for her husband's behavior. Because she took quick action, used good judgment, and spoke wisely, she protected the lives of her family. Later, after Nabal died, David married Abigail.

We are responsible for our choices—good and bad. Likewise, we are not responsible for other people's actions or the situations that they may cause. We can, however, choose to use God's wisdom to make the best of a bad situation. We can choose to do whatever we can do, and leave the rest in God's hands.

When circumstances caused by others are beyond our control, the one thing we can do is trust God and seek His wisdom. He will give us the right direction and the required strength.

I sometimes get frustrated when people who are not serving God make bad choices. Rather than get frustrated and make bad choices, I need to turn the situation over to God and seek His wisdom. He will always grant us wisdom when we ask. And when we seek Him and obey Him, He works all things out for our good.

CHAPTER TEN

2 SAMUEL

(David) won over the hearts of the men of Judah so that they were all of one mind.

2 Samuel 19:14

DAVID THE KING

(2 Samuel Chapters 1–12)

When David heard of the death of Saul and Jonathan,
he tore his clothes and mourned with all his men.
David wrote a lament in his despair
and taught it to his people everywhere.

And finally, after years of waiting,
David was anointed as their king.
He now ruled the tribe of Judah and more.
But between the house of Saul and David, there was still war.

David's kingdom grew stronger over time.
Six sons were born to him through his wives.
Then David sent out this message:
"Bring back Michal to whom I was engaged."

David was again reunited with Michal, his wife.
Then men took Saul's remaining son's life.
David was saddened, and the men were punished.
Then David was king over Israel as God had wished.

David was thirty years old when he became king.
He reigned forty years over everything.
He conquered Jerusalem and made his home there.
The fortress of Zion—called the city of David is where.

He became more powerful because God was with him.
He took more wives and had more children.
He defeated the Philistines when they tried to attack,
and he brought the Ark of the Covenant back.

David offered sacrifices and danced before the Lord
as the people praised God and played chords.
Michal despised David's public display of affection,
but God loved David's worship and adulation.

David defeated Zobah and the Moabites,
the Arameans, and the Edomites.
The Lord gave David victory wherever he went.
He was famous for his achievements.

David wanted to show kindness and kinship
to Jonathan's family for their friendship.
He gave Jonathan's son Mephibosheth
all his father's land and inheritance.

It was time for all the kings to go to war.
David stayed at home and became bored.

As he was walking along the roof of the palace,
he got into trouble and caused malice.

He saw a woman named Bathsheba bathing.
He wanted her because her beauty was amazing.
He sent for her, and they slept together.
Then David received a message from her.

"I am pregnant, and the child is yours," she said.
Then David began to scheme and get ideas in his head.
He tried to trick her husband into sleeping with her.
But Uriah was loyal and stayed with the other soldiers.

So David began to develop another plan:
to have Uriah killed by the enemy's hand.
He put Uriah on the front lines of the fight
and had the rest of the men fall back out of sight.

Uriah died, and Bathsheba mourned for her husband.
Then after a time, she went to the palace, and
David married her. He made her his wife.
But the child they shared lost his life.

David was sad that he had sinned against God.
He turned back to God and was awed.
God blessed them with another son.
The son's name was Solomon.

DAVID THE FATHER

(2 Samuel Chapter 13–24 and 1 Kings Chapter 1–2)

David had many wives and many children.
He had a son whose name was Amnon.
Amnon was in love with Tamar, his half-sister.
He sinned and forced himself on her.

He hated her and threw her out in shame and disgust.
She went to her brother Absalom, who she could trust.
King David was furious but never punished Amnon.
So Absalom killed his father's other son.

Absalom was banished from the kingdom,
but David longed to see his son.
David brought him back but would not see him.
After two years, they were reunited again.

But Absalom was bitter and hated the king.
He rebelled against him and wanted everything.
So David had to flee to a safe place afar
until he was hidden away from harm.

Absalom planned to take over the kingdom
until some of David's men murdered him.
David mourned when he was told;
then he returned back to his home.

The Lord delivered David from his enemy's hand,
so David sang songs of praise to the Lord again.
He won the hearts of the men of Judah,
so they were completely loyal to their ruler.

As David lay sick and frail on his death bed,
he said, "Solomon will be king before I am dead."
The family said their goodbyes with tears.
David ruled over Israel for forty years.

Sidebar: David

A MAN AFTER GOD'S OWN HEART

The account of David and Goliath usually makes us think of the little guy defeating the giant. But it is so much more than that. It is a story of faith, courage, obedience, and God's power to overcome any situation. We can learn some very important life lessons from David.

The first lesson is that we should be standing up for what is right no matter the cost. Our nation—our world—is spinning out of control. Sin is more and more rampant and true believers in Christ are the minority. People are using and abusing the name of God all around us, and we are just sitting down and letting it happen.

David was angry that Goliath had defied the army of the Lord and insulted God Himself. He could not stand by and watch when he knew the power of God. He told Saul that he had defeated lions and bears, and that he would "do it to this pagan Philistine, too, for he has defied the armies of the living God!" He went on to say, "The LORD who rescued me from the claws of the lion and the bear will rescue me from this Philistine" (1 Samuel 17:36 NLT)!

David had no doubt in the power of God. He trusted not in his ability but in the power of God. David placed his trust completely in God for his own safety and for the future of his nation.

Second, David knew that victory over Goliath would show everyone who God was. By facing the giant with the tools he had at hand and "in the name of the LORD of Heaven's armies—the God of the armies of Israel, whom you have defied," David knew that the victory and glory would go to God (1 Samuel 17:45–47 NLT). The victory that David anticipated would demonstrate the existence and power of God.

Third, David's confidence came from his experiences about how the Lord had delivered him in the past. He knew he could trust God because he remembered everything God had done for him.

Fourth, David had spent time with God. The Psalms show us how David kept an open line of communication with God. Sometimes he praised, sometimes he vented, sometimes he cried out to God in anguish, and sometimes he reminded God of all the things He had done and trusted God to keep His Word.

Finally, David was a man after God's own heart. How could a liar, adulterer, and murderer be a man after God's heart? The answer is honesty. He committed some horrible sins, but David's response to his sin was to honestly seek God. He was sorry for his sins. He confessed his sins. He learned from his sins and moved forward. He was sincere in his relationship with God.

Here are the life lessons we can learn from David:

1. Fight the battle first and foremost on our knees. The power to be courageous and victorious comes from an intimate relationship with and knowledge of God. This means time in prayer, praise, and Bible study.

2. Trusting God means having faith—looking past what we can see to what God sees. And God sees far beyond what we can see.

3. God's protection is our defense. With God's protection, we can march with confidence into any battle.

4. Faithful obedience should be our response whenever the Holy Spirit prompts us to go into action. David activated his faith before he activated his will.

5. One way to activate our faith is to recall God's faithfulness in our lives. Just as David remembered God's protection and provision before walking into the valley to confront Goliath, we should recall all the ways God has been faithful and delivered us before facing our challenges. We should remember past victories and how God has been with us to give us courage to face our future.

6. We should have the right attitude and trust God, not ourselves. We mustn't let our fears or circumstances dictate our actions. We must only look to God for the right response.

7. Finally, we should use the resources that God has already given us. Instead of praying for God to give us a special weapon or additional resource, we should allow God to develop and use the gifts, abilities, talents, and resources He has already blessed us with. Not asking for more gives us an opportunity to give Him glory.

Faith is believing that God will do what He has promised. Faith is trusting that God will honor His promises. We can move forward in obedience knowing that God rewards those who trust and obey Him.

We cannot be like the Israelites, responding to Satan's threats with stress reactions, anxious frustration, or paralyzing fear. We, like David, can be confident because we know the battle is the Lord's. He will be victorious.

Instead of focusing on our inability, we should focus on God's infinite ability. It is all about keeping our focus on God and not on our circumstances. It is about doing what we already know how to do, while trusting God to do the rest knowing that God is always faithful to His Word. That is faith in action.

If we are going to be victorious people who stand up for God, then defeat is never an option. Trust, faith, and courage are the only options. We cannot trust the future of our nation to any man or woman. We can only trust God to change hearts and lives, and let Him use us to stand up for Him, and to love the hurting.

> *How amazing are the deeds of the LORD! All who delight in him should ponder them. Everything he does reveals his glory and majesty. His righteousness never fails. He causes us to remember his wonderful works. How gracious and merciful is our LORD!*
>
> *He has shown his great power to his people by giving them the lands of other nations. All he does is just and good, and all his commandments are trustworthy. They are forever true, to be obeyed faithfully and with integrity. He has paid a full ransom for his people. He has guaranteed his covenant with them forever. What a holy, awe-inspiring name he has!*
>
> *Psalm 111:2–4, 6–9 NLT*

CHAPTER ELEVEN

1 KINGS

King Solomon was greater in riches and wisdom than all the other kings of the earth. The whole world sought audience with Solomon to hear the wisdom God had put in his heart.

1 Kings 10:23–24

SOLOMON

(1 Kings Chapters 2–11:42)

Before David died, he gave a charge to his son.
"Be strong and act like a man," he told Solomon.
Solomon made an alliance with Pharaoh, king of Egypt.
He married Pharaoh's daughter and formed an allegiance.

Solomon showed his love for God by obeying.
Then God spoke to Solomon while he was praying.
"I will give you anything you want," God said.
Of all the choices, Solomon chose wisdom instead.

Because Solomon asked for this instead of riches or a long life,
God blessed him with discernment to always know what is right.
God also gave him wealth and honor
and established his kingdom forever.

Solomon's first test of wisdom involved two women
and the living, breathing child that once had been.
One of the babies had died (this was known),
but each mother claimed the remaining child as her own.

Solomon told the soldiers to cut the baby in half.
"Then neither of us will have him," one woman spat.
But the child's real mother was moved with compassion.
"No," she cried. "Let the other woman have him."

The King knew which mother was honest.
He returned the baby to his mother for solace.
Then there was amazement and awe throughout the kingdom,
and people came from all over the world to hear his wisdom.

Solomon began building the temple of the Lord.
He built it exactly as God had foretold.
He built it with the finest cedar wood
and inlaid it with gold, and it was good.

He built an inner sanctuary that was extravagant.
There he placed the Ark of the Covenant.
He made grand doors out of olive wood beams.
It took seven years to build King David's dream.

When the priests brought the Ark into the inner sanctuary,
God's presence fell and the temple was filled with His glory.
Inside the Ark were the stone tablets with God's commandments.
They were a reminder of God's promises and His covenant.

The temple was a place where God's presence dwelled.
The king blessed the people as it was unveiled.

He prayed a prayer of dedication before the mass.
Then King Solomon finished building his palace.

He built ships to explore and to bring back riches.
The kingdom grew and was more ambitious.
The queen of Sheba heard of Solomon's fame.
To test his knowledge, from far away she came.

Solomon answered every question—none were too hard.
The queen esteemed him and held him in high regard.
He was greater in riches and wisdom than any other.
When he died, he had reigned forty years altogether.

KINGS OF ISRAEL

(1 Kings Chapters 11:43–16:28)

After Solomon's death, his son Rehoboam became king.
Rehoboam listened to bad advice, and he was mean.
The kingdom was divided as the people rebelled against Rehoboam.
The other part of the kingdom pledged allegiance to Jeroboam.

Jeroboam sinned and made idols for the people.
He would not change, and his ways were evil.
He did more evil than all the ones before.
He sinned and turned his back on the Lord.

His son Abijah became ill and died.
None of his line would be multiplied.
He reigned for twenty-two years before his death.
His son Nadab filled the hole that was left.

Nadab also did what was evil in God's eyes.
He reigned only two years, then he died.
Baasha killed him and took his throne.
He killed the entire family that was known.

Baasha reigned twenty-four years and was evil.
Then Elah his son ruled and brought more upheaval.
Elah ruled two years and then was overthrown
by Zimri, one of his officials, who took the throne.

Zimri ruled only seven days when his kingdom was taken.
He set the palace on fire around him and left it blazing.
Omri ruled twelve years but also did evil in God's eyes.
Then he was succeeded by his son Ahab upon his demise.

Rehoboam son of Solomon ruled Jerusalem.
He was evil and he caused many problems.
He ruled seventeen years and watched the kingdom degrade.
He watched as the temple treasures were stolen, all Solomon had made.

Then Rehoboam's son Abijah became king.
He was evil and had only a three-year reign.
He committed all the same sins as the others.
His son Asa was a different king altogether.

Asa reigned over Judah for forty-one years.
To God's will and commands, he did adhere.
His heart was fully committed to the Lord.
He got rid of all the idols God abhorred.

King Asa's son Jehoshaphat was king after his death.
He reigned twenty-five years and did good while he had breath.
There was war between the two royal families.
It continued through the years with many casualties.

ELIJAH

(1 Kings Chapters 16:29–19:19a)

Ahab reigned over Israel for twenty-two years.
He was more evil than any of his peers.
He married Jezebel and worshiped Baal.
It was a sin against God—the ultimate betrayal.

There was a prophet of God named Elijah.
He was a good man and was righteous.
He prophesied that there would be a drought.
For several years, God brought it about.

God provided food and water for the prophet
and told him to hide out in the ravine of Kerith.
When the drought caused the brook to run dry,
God told Elijah to go to Sidon by and by.

God said, "There is a widow who will supply you with food."
Elijah saw the widow God spoke of gathering wood.
He asked the woman for a little water and some bread.
"I am preparing a last meal for my son and I," she said.

Elijah told her to go home and to not be afraid.
"Make a small loaf for me and one for yourself," he said.
"God says, 'you will not run out of oil or flour
until I send rain and you see the first shower.'"

There was food every day for all of them to eat.
Sometime later the boy became sick and weak.
The boy finally died, and the woman grieved.
But Elijah prayed to God, and the boy lived.

Ahab's wife Jezebel was killing all the prophets of the Lord.
But Obadiah, the palace administrator, was a follower of God's Word.
He hid a hundred of God's prophets in a cave.
He brought them food and water, and they were saved.

God spoke to Elijah after the third year.
"Go speak to Ahab, and I will send rain here."
Elijah obeyed and found Obadiah,
and told him what had transpired.

Because of Jezebel, Obadiah was distressed,
but he still told Ahab of Elijah's request.

Elijah met with Ahab as God had directed.
He was unafraid because he was protected.

King Ahab accused Elijah of making trouble for Israel.
Elijah told the king, "You have caused all of this trouble.
You have abandoned all of God's commands
and worshipped the idols of the land.

"Now summon all the people to meet on Mount Carmel.
Bring the four hundred and fifty prophets of Baal."
Elijah told the people of Israel to decide:
follow God or Baal—choose a side.

The people refused to say a word,
so Elijah put a test before the Lord.
He made a sacrifice and had Baal's prophets do the same.
Then he told them to call out Baal's name.

Elijah said, "The one true God will answer by fire."
The people replied, "We will do what is required."
The prophets of Baal called out from morning till night.
They shouted, danced, and cut themselves. What a sight!

When Baal did not answer the prophets, Elijah said,
"Shout louder. Maybe he is thinking, busy, or sleeping in bed."
Still Baal did not answer them.
Elijah told the people to come to him.

He repaired God's altar that had been torn down
and dug a trench around the altar in the ground.
He had them pour water on the altar until it filled the trench below.
He prayed to God to answer his prayer so all the people would know,

that God is the One True God above all,
Before Him all other idols will fall.
Then the fire of the Lord came down;
it burnt the sacrifice, the altar, and the ground.

All the people fell facedown and were awed.
They all said, "The Lord—He is God."
Elijah sent Ahab back to his palace.
A cloud began to appear in the vastness.

The sky grew black with clouds and the wind came
as it began to look and feel a lot like rain.
The power of God came upon Elijah, and he ran so fast
that he outran the king's chariot as he passed.

Jezebel heard about the things that took place.
She swore to kill Elijah within the next few days.
Elijah was afraid and ran for his life.
He went into the wilderness to hide.

He prayed for death to the Lord above.
"Lord," he said, "I have had enough!"
Then he lay down under a bush and fell asleep.
An angel touched him and said, "Get up and eat."

There was a jug of water and some baked bread.
So he woke up and ate; then went back to bed.
The angel came a second time and told him to eat
because he had a long journey and needed strength.

Elijah traveled forty days and forty nights
until he reached Horeb—the mountain heights.
He found a cave and spent the night there.
Then the word of God came—an answer to prayer.

"I am the only prophet left," Elijah said.
"And the king and the people of Israel want me dead."
God said, "Go stand on the mountain while my presence passes by,"
as a great and powerful wind blew through from on high.

An earthquake came and then a fire.
But God was not in any of those things that transpired.

After the fire came a gentle whisper.
The presence of God came like a shiver.

Then God asked Elijah, "What are you doing here?"
"They are trying to kill me!" Elijah cried out in fear.
God said, "Go back the way you came to Damascus.
You will anoint two new kings to rule the masses.

"Then anoint Elisha from Abel to succeed you.
He will be the one to step in your shoes."
So Elijah did just as the Lord willed.
He found Elisha out plowing the fields.

AHAB AND JEZEBEL

(1 Kings Chapter 19:19b–2 Kings Chapter 1)

Elijah found Elisha plowing the field and threw his cloak around him.
Elisha ran back to say goodbye to his parents and to kiss them.
He slaughtered his animals and fed the people that dwelled there.
Then he left to follow Elijah and become his helper.

Meanwhile Ben-Hadad prepared to attack Israel.
But a prophet came to King Ahab to foretell.
"You will win this battle," was God's word.
"Then you will know that I am the Lord."

So Ahab's army attacked Ben-Hadad and all his allies,
while they were getting drunk, and caused their demise.
But Ben-Hadad escaped on horseback and fled with some of his men.
The prophet told Ahab, "Strengthen your army. He will attack again."

The Israelites defeated the other army again.
Ben-Hadad fled with some of his men.
He decided to meet with Ahab and to beg for mercy.
Ahab granted his request and made a treaty.

There was a vineyard that belonged to Naboth close to the palace.
Ahab wanted it and asked Naboth to give it up as they discussed.

Naboth refused to turn it over, so the king went home to pout.
But Jezebel, Ahab's wife, had Naboth killed after being thrown out.

Jezebel told Ahab about Naboth's demise,
so he went to the vineyard to claim his prize.
But Elijah found Ahab there, and he said,
"God says, 'Because of your sin, you will be dead.'"

Elijah told Ahab that Jezebel would also die.
In their sins, they had gone completely awry.
There was no one before as evil as Ahab,
urged on by his wife Jezebel, who was bad.

When Ahab heard these words, he lamented.
He sought mercy from God, and God relented.
God said, "Ahab will not die today."
So Ahab left and went on his way.

Jehoshaphat, King of Judah, went to see King Ahab.
He wanted to join together and attack Ramoth-Gilead.
The kings called on Micaiah the prophet, out of curiosity,
to call on God to see if they would have victory.

All the other prophets said what the king wanted to hear,
But Micaiah said, "You will lose. The end is near."
King Ahab was so angry that he threw Micaiah into prison.
He said, "Give him only bread and water until my disposition."

During the battle, Ahab was mortally wounded by an archer's hand.
Then a cry spread throughout the army, "Every man to his land!"
Ahab the king died just as the word of the Lord declared.
Ahaziah his son succeeded him as king and as heir.

Ahaziah, the son of Ahab, also did evil in the eyes of the Lord.
He followed the ways of his parents, whose ways God abhorred.
He died when he fell through the upper room of his lair.
Then Joram succeeded him as king, since he had no heir.

CHAPTER TWELVE

2 KINGS

As they were walking along and talking together, suddenly a chariot of fire and horses of fire appeared and separated the two of them, and Elijah went up to Heaven in a whirlwind.

2 Kings 2:11

ELISHA

(2 Kings Chapters 2–13)

After Elijah found Elisha, and they were on their way from Gilgal, Elijah said, "Stay here. The Lord has sent me to Bethel." Elisha refused to stay and said, "I will not leave you," because he knew the thing that God was about to do.

The company of prophets had asked Elisha "You know the Lord is going to take Elijah?" Many more times Elijah told Elisha to stay, but Elisha refused and would not go away.

Elijah and Elisha traveled to the Jordan River and waited.
Elijah struck the water with his cloak and the water abated.
As fifty prophets watched and stood around,
the water parted, they walked across on dry ground.

Elijah asked Elisha, "What can I do? Let me hear it."
Elisha said, "I want a double portion of your spirit."
Elijah said, "You have asked a difficult thing,
yet it will be yours when I am ready to leave."

Then a chariot and horses of fire separated them,
and Elijah was taken up to Heaven in a whirlwind.
The spirit of Elijah now rested on Elisha's head.
Elisha became the prophet of Israel instead.

Ahab's son Joram became king of Israel in Samaria.
He was also evil but not as bad as his parents were.
The king of Moab rebelled against the king of Israel.
Joram asked the king of Judah to join him if able.

After they marched together for seven days,
they had no more water, causing delays.
As before, Jehoshaphat suggested finding a prophet of the Lord.
Because of Elisha's respect for Jehoshaphat, he gave them this word:

"Without wind or rain, God will fill this valley with water,
and Moab will be delivered into your hands and slaughtered."
The next morning, the valley was filled with water to drink,
and as prophesied, the Moabites were beaten in a blink.

The wife of one of the prophets came to Elisha for aid.
"My husband is dead and we are in debt," she said.
Elisha asked her, "What do you have in your house?"
"Just a little olive oil," she said after looking around.

Elisha told the widow to go borrow as many jars as she could.
"Fill each jar until it is full, then set to the side if you would."

2 KINGS

So they filled up every jar until there were no more left.
Then the oil stopped flowing, and they were blessed.

Elisha performed many more miracles in the name of God.
His fame was renowned, and many people were awed.
He raised the dead to life and made poisonous food safe.
He fed a hundred men with twenty loaves of bread from grain.

The captain of the king's armies was healed of leprosy when,
(at the advice of Elisha), he bathed seven times in the Jordan.
Elisha made an ax-head float, trapped an army, and ended a famine.
All these things he did with God's power and spirit in him.

When the king of Aram was at war with Israel
whatever plans the king made, God would quell.
The king was enraged and sent troops to capture him.
The troops surrounded the city to apprehend them.

When Elisha's servant got up early the next morning,
he came to Elisha terrified and gave him a warning.
Elisha said, "Don't worry," and asked God to open his eyes.
Then the servant could see, all around them, the angel allies.

During Elisha's time, many kings ruled—both good and bad.
Hazael became king of Israel when he murdered Ben-Hadad.
Jehoram, son of Jehoshaphat, became king of Judah inherent.
He was also evil and followed in the footsteps of his parents.

Elisha sent a prophet to find Jehu, a commander.
He anointed Jehu as king—no longer a bystander.
He said, "You will destroy the house of Ahab and end their line.
God will avenge the blood of the prophets shed by Jezebel, in time."

Jehu defeated Ahaziah and Joram, the two kings of Israel.
Then Jezebel was killed: pushed out of a window at Jezreel.
The rest of Ahab's family was killed just as God had spoken.
The priests of Baal were killed, and all the idols were broken.

Jehu died, and Jehoahaz (his son) became the king.
Meanwhile, Joash (son of Ahaziah) had not been seen.
He was hidden in the temple to stay safe for six years.
Then Jehoiada the priest anointed him king, to cheers.

Joash was seven years old when he began to reign.
He ruled Judah for forty years as their king.
The covenant was restored between God and His people.
King Joash began repairing and rebuilding the temple.

Joash did good in the eyes of the Lord during his reign.
When he died, his son Amaziah became Judah's king.
Jehoahaz (son of Jehu) became king over Israel.
But he also did all of the things that were evil.

When Jehoahaz died, his son Jehoash became king.
He did evil in God's eyes and had a sixteen-year reign.
When Jehoash died, Jeroboam II succeeded his father.
He did evil in God's sight just like many of the others.

Meanwhile, Elisha died and was mourned and buried.
When Amaziah died, his son Azariah was only sixteen.
King Azariah rebuilt Elath and restored it to Judah.
He did all the things that were right on God's agenda.

Sidebar: Naaman

SURRENDER

2 Kings 5:1–15 recalls the account of Naaman. He was commander of the king's army. He was considered a great man and highly regarded, but he had a serious problem. Verse 1 says "He was a valiant soldier, but he had leprosy." One of his servants told him about the prophet Elisha. Naaman told the king and the king insisted that Naaman go see Elisha, and the king even sent a letter with Naaman on his behalf.

How important Naaman must have felt approaching Elisha's house with his horses and chariots and his king's approval and how humiliated

Naaman might have felt when Elisha did not immediately come to personally heal him. Instead Elisha sent a messenger to tell Naaman to go wash himself seven times in the Jordan and his flesh would be restored, he would be cleansed.

So Naaman did what we usually do when God doesn't answer our prayers the way we think He should. He went away angry and disappointed. He wondered why God would want him to wash in the dirty Jordan. This is what Naaman said before going away angry.

> *I thought that he would surely come out to me and stand and call on the name of the Lord his God, wave his hand over the spot and cure me of my leprosy. Are not Abana and Pharpar, the rivers of Damascus, better than all the waters of Israel? Couldn't I wash in them and be cleansed?*
>
> *2 Kings 5:11–12*

Thankfully, Naaman had brave and wise servants who went to him and said,

> *My father, if the prophet had told you to do some great thing, would you not have done it? How much more, then, when he tells you, "Wash and be cleansed"!*
>
> *2 Kings 5:13*

So Naaman obeyed the word of God spoken through the prophet Elisha. He "dipped himself in the Jordan seven times, as the man of God had told him, and his flesh was restored and became clean like that of a young boy" (2 Kings 5:14). Then Naaman knew that there was no other God than the one true God.

Humility is not the same thing as humiliation. God may allow us to face circumstances beyond our control, not to humiliate us, but to humble us, to draw us closer to Him, to teach us, to show us who He is, or to refresh and renew us spiritually. We may feel entitled because we have "done everything right." We may consider ourselves a "good person." We might even think we are too good to do the seemingly menial task that God has asked us to do. We may just feel overwhelmed and exhausted by the enemy's attacks. No matter what we feel or think, when we don't understand or have all the answers, we can always trust God and surrender to Him.

> *"Blessed is the one who trusts in the Lord, whose confidence is in him. They will be like a tree planted by the water....It does not fear when heat comes;...It has no worries in a year of drought and never fails to bear fruit."*
>
> Jeremiah 17:7-8

God is our hope and strength. And hope never disappoints. (Romans 5:5). We can place our confidence in Him without fear. Surrendering to God brings confidence and assurance of God's goodness. Surrendering to God brings rest and renewal. We can find physical rest for our bodies but only God can give us rest for our souls.

> *"Come to me, all you who are weary and burdened, and I will give you rest....learn from me,...for you will find rest for your souls."*
>
> Matthew 11:28-29

God can only show goodness and mercy because that is Who He is!

HEZEKIAH AND THE REST OF THE KINGS OF JUDAH
(2 Kings Chapters 14–25)

King Azariah of Judah was succeeded by his son Jotham.
Zechariah became king of Israel after the death of Jeroboam.
Zechariah was evil and only ruled for six months,
He was assassinated by the next king, Shallum.

Shallum ruled one month before he was assassinated.
Menahem, his killer, took over after he was incapacitated.
Menahem ruled ten years and was an evil pariah.
He was succeeded by his son, Pekahiah.

Pekahiah reigned only two years, then he was assassinated by Pekah.
Pekah was evil and reigned twenty years then was killed by Hoshea.
In Judah, King Jotham did what was good in God's eyes.
Jotham reigned for sixteen years before he died.

Jotham was succeeded by his son Ahaz, who reigned for sixteen years.
Ahaz did what was evil in God's sight and sacrificed his son in the fires.
He was succeeded by his son Hezekiah, who did right in God's sight.
Hezekiah ruled twenty-nine years and trusted in God and His might.

There was no one else like Hezekiah among the other kings.
God was with him, and he was successful in everything.
King Hoshea was the last king of Israel in Samaria.
He was defeated, and the Israelites were deported to Assyria.

Israel was exiled because of their sin and idolatry.
They turned their backs on God and His majesty.
Hezekiah, king of Judah, prayed to God for deliverance
as the Assyrian Kings prepared to attack with irreverence.

Just as the prophet Isaiah had prophesied to Hezekiah,
the Assyrians were defeated and their king fled to Nineveh.
Hezekiah became ill, and he was about to die.
He prayed that his death would not draw nigh.

God healed Hezekiah and added fifteen years to his life.
God promised the king He would save the city from strife.
Hezekiah had many more accomplishments during his reign
He started a revival and rebuilt a shattered nation again.

When Hezekiah died, his son Manesseh began his royal career.
He was twelve years old and reigned for fifty-five years.
He did not follow the ways of his father,
but he did evil as had so many others.

Amon succeeded his father Manesseh as king,
but he also did many evil things.

King Amon was murdered by his people.
His son Josiah was next in the line of regals.

Josiah was eight when he began his monarchy.
He reigned thirty-one years and ruled honestly.
He continued to work to have the temple built.
He found the Books of the Law and was filled with guilt.

God promised Josiah that he would not see the punishment
that the people would see because they broke the covenant.
Josiah read aloud the Books of the Law and all its words,
then he renewed the covenant between them and the Lord.

There was not another king who turned to the Lord like he did.
When he died, his son Jehoahaz became king, but he sinned.
Jehoiakim became king when Jehoahaz was carried off by Pharaoh.
Jehoiakim also did evil in God's eyes and caused much sorrow.

When Jehoiakim died, his evil son Jehoiachin became the next king.
He surrendered to King Nebuchadnezzar when Jerusalem was seized.
Nebuchadnezzar took the treasures from the temple and meanwhile
carried ten thousand of the people of Jerusalem into exile.

Jehoiachin's uncle, Zedekiah, was made king in his place.
He also did evil and turned away from God's face.
Finally, as predicted by the prophets, Jerusalem fell,
and all of Judah went into captivity as well.

Sidebar: The Tribe of Dan

SLIPPING INTO IDOLATRY

In Joshua, Judges, 1 Kings, and 2 Kings, we see the account of the tribe of Dan. Although they were promised by covenant their God-given inheritance (the land of Canaan), they never received it because they did not trust God and they took matters into their own hands. They spied on and slaughtered a peaceful city. Then they rebelled further by taking the priest and the idols with them. King Jeroboam then built altars and made idols in places that were significant and convenient for them to worship, replacing the living God with idols of dead gods. Idolatry led to other types of sin and rebellion. Eventually, rebellion led them back into captivity.

In Judges 2:1–3 God promises to lead the Israelites out of captivity and into Canaan. God says He will never break His covenant with them and tells them to not make a covenant with the people of that land and to break down their altars. God gives them this warning: "I will not drive them out before you; they will become traps for you, and their gods will become snares to you" (Judges 2:3).

God's warning was not a threat. It was a natural consequence of their actions. When we make other things more important than heeding His Word and obeying God's covenants, we fail.

Sometimes we take the easy way out instead of standing up for God. Sometimes we tell ourselves It's just not worth it. Christianity is not convenient. When we refuse to stand up for God, neglect our worship of Him or let others talk us into taking the easier path instead of trusting God, we open the door for rebellion and idolatry. When God is no longer number one in our lives, something or someone else certainly will take His place.

Like the tribe of Dan, the more we conform instead of transform, the more we will take on the characteristics of the ungodly and imitate the godlessness around us. Romans 12:2 says,

> *Do not conform to the pattern of this world, but be transformed by the renewing of your mind. Then you will be able to test and approve what God's will is—his good, pleasing and perfect will.*

We must renew our minds daily with time spent in prayer and in the Word, so that we can know God's will and not conform to the sinful pattern of this world. If we do not reclaim this nation for God, it will become a pagan nation.

> *My sheep listen to my voice; I know them, and they follow me. I give them eternal life, and they shall never perish; no one will snatch them out of my hand. My Father, who has given them to me, is greater than all; no one can snatch them out of my Father's hand.*
> John 10:27–29

Christians can fall into sin, repent of it and turn from that sin and back to God. No one can take us from Him. However, the Bible also says, "rebellion is like the sin of divination, and arrogance like the evil of idolatry" causing God to reject us (1 Samuel 15:23).

This is God's first commandment.

> *I am the Lord your God, who brought you out of Egypt, out of the land of slavery. You shall have no other gods before me.*
> Exodus 20:2–3

Idolatry is a slippery slope. The devil tells us lies and tries to deceive us into believing that one sin is not as bad as another. But God does not qualify sin. In His eyes, sin is sin. Even the smallest sin can lead us away from the cross of Christ and toward idols.

God's mercy and patience with us are beyond our ability to comprehend. He pursues us until we respond to Him. But sometimes rebellion or a hard heart makes us unreachable. I believe we can turn so far away from God in our stubbornness that we place ourselves out of His reach. Our hearts can turn completely away from Him if we let them. Hebrews 3:12–15 says:

> *See to it, brothers and sisters, that none of you has a sinful, unbelieving heart that turns away from the living God. But encourage one another daily, as long as it is called "Today," so that none of you may be hardened by sin's deceitfulness. We have come to share in Christ, if indeed we hold our original conviction firmly to the very end. As has just been said: 'Today, if you hear his voice, do not harden your hearts as you did in the rebellion.'*

2 KINGS

I am so thankful for God's mercy, grace, and patience for all the times I fell into sin. I am so grateful that He never stopped chasing me no matter how far I fell.

CHAPTER THIRTEEN

1 AND 2 CHRONICLES

The priests and the Levites stood to bless the people, and God heard them, for their prayer reached Heaven, his holy dwelling place.

2 Chronicles 30:27

CHRONICLES

(1 Chronicles Chapters 1–29 and 2 Chronicles Chapters 1–36)

This is the genealogy of the children of Israel
from Adam to Noah after mankind fell.
The lineage continued with Abraham, Isaac, and Jacob,
and the chronicles of the kings starting with David.

Solomon (son of David) asked for wisdom
establishing himself firmly over his kingdom.
He built the temple of David's dreams,
and his wisdom and wealth were his fame.

Israel rebelled against Rehoboam as king,
then Israel and Judah were divided from within.
This is the history of the kings of Israel and Judah:
from King Rehoboam to the reforms of King Asa.

Jehoshaphat had great wealth and honor.
He appointed both judges and scholars.
Elijah the prophet was taken to Heaven in a whirlwind,
and Jehoiada the priest saved Joash the future king.

Uzziah, whose fame spread to the borders of Egypt,
was well-known as powerful, good, and decent.
Jotham also walked with God and was powerful.
Hezekiah restored the temple and celebrated festivals.

The Lord listened to Hezekiah and healed the people.
They praised the Lord, rejoiced, and were gleeful.
Hezekiah prepared the storerooms for the tithes.
He built aqueducts to keep the enemy dry.

Josiah found the Books of the Law and set the temple in order.
Jerusalem fell because in God they had lost their fervor.
The temple and the city were burnt to the ground,
and the children of God were carried away and bound.

CHAPTER FOURTEEN

EZRA

Ezra came up from Babylon. He was a teacher well versed in the Law of Moses, which the Lord, the God of Israel, had given. The king had granted him everything he asked, for the hand of the Lord his God was on him.

Ezra 7:6

EZRA

(Ezra Chapters 1–10)

In the first year of the reign of Cyrus (king of Persia),
God moved in his heart and gave him courage
to build a temple for the Lord in Jerusalem.
So he gathered up silver and gold in Judah.

Some of the captives from Babylon
brought freewill gifts to act upon.
The priests began to build the altar of the Lord
in accordance with what was written in the Word.

The people began to bring their sacrifices to the altar they made,
even though the foundation of the temple had not yet been laid.
They gave money to the carpenters and masons and began the work.
They sang praises and songs of thanksgiving to the Lord.

The enemies of Israel tried to stop the building of the temple.
The king issued an order to cease; the work came to a standstill.
Haggai and Zechariah (two prophets) began the work again.
Once again the enemies of Israel tried to stop the men.

This time the builders were allowed to continue with pleasantry.
The king decreed the costs were to be paid by the royal treasury.
King Darius told no one to lift a finger against the builders.
He said punishment would come to anyone who hinders.

So the people of Israel finished the temple with elation.
They celebrated with joy and sacrifices of dedication.
The Lord changed the mind and attitude of the king of Assyria,
so that he helped them build the house of the God of Israel.

Ezra, a teacher well versed in the law of Moses,
came up from Babylon on the king's notice.
Ezra devoted himself to the study of God's Word,
and he was full of the Spirit of the Lord.

He found favor with Artaxerxes the king
and brought up riches and other things.
Ezra interceded before the Lord again
on behalf of the people who had sinned.

The people were so overwhelmed with guilt;
They wept before the temple that was built.
They came to Ezra and made a vow
to follow God—right here and now.

CHAPTER FIFTEEN

NEHEMIAH

When I heard these things, I sat down and wept. For some days I mourned and fasted and prayed before the God of Heaven.

Nehemiah 1:4

NEHEMIAH

(Nehemiah Chapters 1–13)

While Nehemiah was in the citadel of Susa,
he asked about the exiles and Jerusalem.
When he heard that the wall was broken down,
he wept as he sat down on the ground.

Nehemiah fasted and prayed for several days
asking God to forgive them for their evil ways.
He praised God for His goodness and faithfulness
and reminded God of His words and graciousness.

Nehemiah was cupbearer to the king,
so he asked God for favor to be seen.
Nehemiah took the king his wine as usual.
The king wondered why Nehemiah was miserable.

Nehemiah said, "How can I not be distressed?"
"The city I love is in ruins," he expressed.
The king asked Nehemiah, "How can I ease your pain?"
Nehemiah responded, "Let us build up the wall again."

Nehemiah also asked for letters from the king
for safe travel, timber, and beams.
Because God showed Nehemiah gracious favor,
the king granted his requests without waiver.

There were some officials who were against the restoration.
They did not want to see the wall rebuilt or the renovation.
Nehemiah found some people who were ready to build,
though some of the people ridiculed them still.

Nehemiah did not worry but looked ahead.
"The God of Heaven will give us success," he said.
The dissenters mocked the builders to their face
as Nehemiah prayed and the repairs got under way.

Half of the men were posted as guards
to watch the builders with spears and swords.
Nehemiah continued to encourage the people,
"Our God will fight for us against the evil."

Nehemiah devoted himself to work on the wall.
The completed wall took fifty-two days in all.
The priests and the gatekeepers, the musicians and the Levites,
and the temple servants settled in their towns with the Israelites.

Ezra the teacher brought out the Books of the Law.
He read it from morning till noon in front of them all.

NEHEMIAH

All the people listened attentively,
as the book was read before the assembly.

Ezra opened the book and all the people stood
to show their reverence because the Lord is good.
The people cried as they heard the Word.
They repented, and they praised the Lord.

Because Nehemiah's heart was broken,
he became determined and outspoken.
His agony and holy fervor for God's people
led to the rebuilding of the wall and the temple.

WRECK MY HEART

(Inspired by the Book of Nehemiah)

Awesome and mighty God, wreck my heart.
From the depths of my soul, I am torn apart.
You have rescued me from my addiction and my sin.
You've taken the hurt, pain, and anger from within.

Filled with Your love, compassion, and fire,
it has become my deepest and best desire
to carry Your love and hope to the one,
whose life is torn apart by addiction and undone.

You are the only One who can truly heal
our hearts so full of fear, and still
take the hurt, anger, shame, and guilt.
Crash down the walls we have built.

Wreck our hearts, O God, for the lost.
We surrender to you, no matter the cost.
In this vapor of a life, let us truly see
the important things will last eternally.

CHAPTER SIXTEEN

ESTHER

Who knows but that you have come to your royal position for such a time as this?

Esther 4:14

ESTHER

(Esther Chapters 1–10)

King Xerxes ruled from Susa in the citadel.
A banquet for all the people was held.
The king generously shared with his subjects.
For the women, there was another banquet.

The king's personal attendants had a proposition:
"Let finding you a beautiful bride be our new mission."
All the beautiful young women were brought before the king.
A woman named Esther pleased him more than anything.

Esther was a Jew and the cousin of Mordecai.
Mordecai raised her after being carried into exile.
Esther was beautiful and won the favor of everyone who saw her.
King Xerxes loved Esther and made her queen above the others.

One day Mordecai heard a plot to overthrow the king.
The plot was foiled when Esther revealed everything.
Later an evil man named Haman was promoted to power.
He was arrogant and vain, but Mordecai refused to cower.

Mordecai's defiance angered Haman so severely
that he wanted to destroy all the Jews sincerely.
Haman plotted against the Jews and came up with a story.
He told the king things about them that were accusatory.

The King ordered that the Jews be destroyed.
To carry out the orders, dispatches were deployed.
When Mordecai heard, he tore his clothes in sorrow.
He asked his cousin Esther to speak to the king tomorrow.

Esther told Mordecai that she could not approach the king unless summoned.
Mordecai replied, "Being queen doesn't mean that you are safe, my cousin.
Deliverance will come from God, one way or another.
How do you know God does not have a plan for you, Esther?

"God may have put you right here, right now,
to save your people the Jews somehow."
Esther had all the Jews and Mordecai fast and pray.
Then she approached the king after three days.

The king was glad to see Esther and let her approach.
He was willing to give her anything that she chose.
Esther asked if she could prepare a banquet and invite Haman.
The king agreed, and they began the banquet celebration.

Haman was delighted until he saw Mordecai at the gate.
Then once again he was angry and full of hate.

ESTHER

He planned to ask the king to impale the Jew Mordecai
at the second banquet Esther prepared the next night.

That same night the king could not sleep,
so he ordered the book of history to read.
The king read how Mordecai had saved him from being killed,
and asked what honor had been given to this man of great zeal.

The king's attendants answered him, "Nothing has been done."
The king ordered Haman to honor Mordecai in front of everyone.
Haman did as the king had said then returned home.
Though grieved, he was called back as the banquet had begun.

Again, the king asked what he could do for the queen.
The queen replied, "Grant me my life—this is my plea.
My people and I are about to be destroyed."
"Who would do such a thing?" he asked annoyed.

When Esther revealed that Haman was the threat,
the king ordered that he be put to death.
On the pole made for Mordecai, Haman was impaled.
Mordecai received the king's signet ring and all that entailed.

Esther asked the king to overrule the orders to kill the Jews.
The king told Mordecai to write new orders "as seems best to you."
Then Mordecai sealed the orders with the signet ring.
He wore the royal garments and crown of the king.

The Jews enjoyed a time of happiness and celebration,
and Mordecai was feared and respected by his nation.
The Jews struck down all their enemies with the sword.
They set aside two days every year in remembrance to the Lord.

Mordecai was second in command to the king,
and Esther saved a nation from being extinct.
God placed Esther in the right place and time,
so she could do God's will and let His glory shine.

SECTION THREE

Major Prophets

CHAPTER SEVENTEEN

ISAIAH

I will not forget you!
See, I have engraved you on the palms of my hands. (God)
Isaiah 49:15–16

ISAIAH THE PROPHET

(Isaiah Chapters 1–66)

These are the messages of the prophet Isaiah
during the reigns of the kings of Judah.
God showed Isaiah what was going to happen to His people in the days ahead.
"The children I loved and cared for have turned against me," God said.

No matter what I do for them, they don't care.
Oh, what a sinful nation they are!
They have turned their backs on me and have despised the Holy One.
They have cut themselves off from my help. They just haven't had enough.

Will you forever rebel? Listen to the Lord and hear what I say.
Don't bring me any empty sacrifices—just please obey.
Sacrifices don't matter when there is no sorrow for sin.
Stop now! I want nothing more to do with them.

Quit your evil ways. Learn to do good and to be fair.
Learn to help the widows, the fatherless, and the poor.
Come, let us talk this over, says the Lord.
I, the Lord, have spoken, so listen to my words.

No matter how dirty your sins have made you feel, I will wash you white as snow.
Even if you are stained as red as crimson, I will cleanse and make you whole.
I want to help you if you let me and only obey me.
But if you don't, you will be killed by your enemies.

Those who return to the Lord, who are just and good, shall be redeemed.
But rebellious sinners shall perish for they refuse to come to me.
These sinners are not even ashamed; they have doomed themselves.
But the godly man will be rewarded; for him all will be well.

I, the Lord, wanted Israel to show justice, but found bloodshed.
I wanted righteousness, but met deep oppression instead.
They have no thought for me or for what I have done for them.
Because of their evil, I will send my people into exile again.

"Then the proud will be humbled and brought down to dust.
But the Lord will be exalted above all; He is holy, good, and just.
The year King Uzziah died I saw the Lord sitting on His throne,"
Isaiah said. "The temple was filled with His glory for He is God alone."

The Lord God was surrounded by angels singing this chorus:
Holy, holy, holy is the Lord Almighty. The earth is filled with his glory.
Their singing shook the temple to its foundations,
and the entire sanctuary was filled with smoke and vapor.

Then I said, "My fate is sealed because I am a sinner,
yet I have seen the Lord of Heaven's armies. He is here."

ISAIAH

One of the angels touched my lips with a burning coal
and said, "Now you are forgiven and made whole."

Then the Lord asked, "Whom shall I send to reach my people?
Who will go?" And I said, "Here I am, Lord. Send me. I will!"
God said, "Go tell my people, *though you hear God's words, you don't understand.*"
They will not listen until they are taken away and their home is a wasteland.

HOPE FOR THE FUTURE
(Isaiah Chapters 1–66)

This is what God told Isaiah during the reign of King Ahaz:
"Your enemies will not succeed, but you can trust my plans.
This is a sign of things to come: a child will be born to a virgin!
His name *Immanuel* (meaning God is with us), she will call him."

The Lord told Isaiah, "Make an announcement that I am giving you a boy,
His name means 'Your enemies will soon be destroyed.'
Maher-shalal-hash-baz—in all capital letters, write his name."
Then Isaiah's wife became pregnant, and their baby boy came.

Isaiah said, "Enemies of Israel, you will not succeed
because God is with us, and He is our safety."
"Write down all these things I am going to do," said the Lord,
and seal them up for the future and pass down my words."

"I will wait for the Lord to help us," said Isaiah.
"My only hope is in the Lord God, Jehovah."
The enemies of Israel will soon be destroyed, says the Lord.
Jehovah will save His people, a remnant will come back as before.

My people will be led away captive and stumbling;
they will be desperate, weary, and hungry.
They will curse God and shake their fists at Heaven,
but the time of darkness will not last forever.

In the future, these lands will be filled with glory.
Israel will again be great and filled with joy.
God will break the chains that bind His people
in that glorious day of peace with no more battles.

For unto us, a son is given; a child is born.
And the government shall be upon His arms.
He will be called The Mighty God, Wonderful,
Everlasting Father, Prince of Peace, and Counselor.

He will rule with perfect fairness and justice from David's throne.
He will bring true justice and peace to all the nations and will be known.
I will not help unjust judges and those who issue unfair laws
Woe to those who give no justice to the poor, orphans, or widows.

Although the royal line of David will be removed,
from the stump will grow a new branch—a shoot.
The Spirit of the Lord will rest upon Him,
and His delight will be His obedience.

The earth will be filled with the knowledge of the Lord.
He will be a banner of salvation to all the world.
But Babylon, once the most glorious of kingdoms, the oppressor of my people
will be brought down and utterly destroyed to never rise again, for their evil.

O Lucifer, son of the morning, how you have fallen from Heaven.
You tried to overthrow God but were removed from His presence.
You were brought down to the pit of hell, down to its lowest depths.
You, who were once mighty, have now become the king of death.

In love a throne will be established; in faithfulness a man will sit on it.
It is the man who seeks justice and righteousness from the house of David.
But you have forgotten God your Savior—your Rock.
So all of your work and plans will come to naught.

Isaiah prophesied against Moab, Damascus, and Egypt: all would be desolation.

ISAIAH

You have forgotten God your Savior, your Rock, and your fortress, you evil nation.
In that day, there will be an altar to the Lord in the heart of Egypt: a monument at its borders.
It will be a sign that the Lord Almighty will save your sons and daughters.

Isaiah prophesied against Edom, Arabia, and the Valley of Vision
to Tyre and the ships of Tarshish, *God has made His decision.*
But the Lord will wipe away the tears from your face;
He will remove from the earth, His people's disgrace.

The people will say, "Surely this is our God. We trusted in Him, and He saved us.
This is the sovereign Lord, let us rejoice and be glad in His salvation."
They will sing this song in Judah, those who are rescued:
You will keep in perfect peace those who trust in You.

"Trust in the Lord, the Rock eternal, the Upright One.
We wait for You God Almighty, our hearts are undone."
Then Isaiah said, *"My soul yearns for You in the night,*
and my spirit longs for You, Lord, in the morning light."

The Lord says, *I will lay down a cornerstone in Zion, and a sure foundation.*
The one who trusts in Him never has to fear for he will find salvation.
I will make righteousness the plumb line and justice the measuring tape.
Listen and hear my voice; pay attention and hear what I say.

These people come near to me with their mouth and honor me with their lips,
but their hearts are far from me; their worship is a bag of tricks.
Once more I will astound these people with my wonders; their wisdom will perish.
They cannot hide their plans from me and their intelligence will vanish.

Woe to my obstinate and rebellious children heaping sin upon sin.
It will become like a high wall that shatters and crashes in.
Your salvation is found in repentance and rest.
Your strength is found in trust and quietness.

"The Lord longs to be gracious to you and show you compassion,"
Isaiah said.
"He is a God of justice and those who wait for Him will be blessed.
He will be gracious to you, and you will no longer weep.
He will answer you as soon as He hears you speak,

No matter where you go, His voice says, *This is the way; walk in it.*
Be strong, do not fear; until you are saved, your God will never quit.
Water will gush forth in the wilderness and streams in the desert.
The grass withers and the flowers die, but God's Word lasts forever.

The Sovereign Lord comes with power, and he rules with a mighty arm.
Lift up your eyes and look to the One who created all the stars.
He brings them out one by one and calls them each by name.
He is the everlasting God, creator of the universe before it became.

He gives strength to the weary, and the weak He makes strong.
People may grow tired and weary, or they may stumble and fall,
but those who hope in the Lord will renew their strength—like eagles they will soar.
They will run and not grow tired; they will walk and faint no more.

GOD'S CHOSEN

(Isaiah Chapters 1–66)

"I have chosen you," the Lord said, "so do not be afraid.
I am with you and I am your God, so do not be dismayed.
I will strengthen you, help you, and hold you up with my righteous right hand.
I am the Lord God who says to you, *Do not fear, I will help you stand.*

I have redeemed you and called you by name because you are Mine.
When you pass through the flood waters, I am with you and you will be fine.
When you walk through the fire, you will not burn and the flames will not ignite.
I am God, the Holy One of Israel, your Savior; you are precious in my sight.

ISAIAH

Do you not see that I am doing a new thing?
In the wasteland, I am making a stream.
I am the God who blots out your sins and remembers them no more.
My Spirit will fall on your children and my blessings I will pour.

I am your King and Redeemer, the Lord God Almighty.
I am the first and the last; there is no God beside me.
I made you and swept away your sins like the dust.
I have redeemed you, so return to me—you must!

You will be a light so that my salvation is available to everyone.
I am your Redeemer, the Holy One of Israel, the Lord of Heaven above.
I have engraved you on the palms of my hands.
You will never be disappointed with my plans.

How precious is the messenger who brings good news of peace.
He proclaims salvation and hope to the captives, and release.
God's saving power came in the form of a servant, lowly and meek.
He had no beauty or majesty to attract us to him—nothing unique.

He was rejected by mankind, a man of suffering and pain.
He was despised by us, and we held Him in low esteem.
Still He took all our pain and bore our suffering.
He was punished and became a sin offering.

But He was wounded, bruised, and crushed for us, punished by God's will.
He was beaten to bring us peace, and because of His wounds, we are healed.
All of us have strayed like sheep from the Shepherd, to follow our own way, running around.
Yet He paid the price for our sins, and like a lamb to the slaughter, never made a sound.

He was led away to His death, and murdered like a criminal.
He was buried in a rich man's tomb but without a funeral.
This was all God's good and perfect will to bring us eternal, abundant life.
Because of His sacrifice, He was given the highest honors on High.

THE BIBLE IN POETRY

God says, *Come, all who are thirsty, to the waters, eat, and drink.*
Listen to me and take what is good, and you will delight in me.
Come to me, the Holy One, and listen that you may live.
I will make an everlasting covenant with you and forgive.

Seek the Lord while He may be found; call on Him while He is close by.
Let the wicked forsake their ways and turn their thoughts to things on high.
He will have mercy, and you will be led out and go forth in peace and gladness.
For my thoughts and ways are higher than yours, the Lord says.

The words that come out of my mouth will not return empty.
They will accomplish the purpose that I desire and see.
Maintain justice, always do the right thing, and to me, yield,
for my salvation is near and my righteousness will soon be revealed.

I live in my holy place with those people who have a broken and contrite spirit,
to revive their spirits and hearts, and to heal and restore my dearest.
I will strengthen you, and your light will break through like the dawn, and you will be healed.
I will answer when you call and satisfy you in a sun-scorched land if you do my will.

The Lord's arm is not too short to save. His ear is not too deaf to hear.
It is your sins and rebellion that have separated you from God's ear.
We walk in shadows and darkness looking for the light.
Our sins testify against us; our offenses are many in God's sight.

The Lord looked and saw that there was no justice and no one to intervene,
so He sent the Redeemer and His own Spirit to forever make us clean.
Arise and shine for the Light has come, and the glory of the Lord is upon you.
You will shine bright like the sun, and your heart will swell with life anew.

I will make you the everlasting pride and joy of all generations.
You will know that I, the Lord, your Redeemer, am your Savior.
I will be your everlasting light because you are Mine,
God says. *Your days of mourning will end in due time.*

ISAIAH

God has given me His spirit and anointed me
to proclaim good news to the poor and to set the captives free.
He has sent me to bind up those who are brokenhearted
and to release those prisoners who are trapped in darkness.

He has sent me to proclaim the year of the Lord's favor and grace
to comfort all who mourn and whose hearts ache,
and to bestow a crown of beauty for ashes and joy, instead of mourning.
For your disgrace and despair, you will rejoice and receive a double portion.

I will hold out my hands to obstinate people who pursue their evil desires.
I will rejoice and delight in my people who cry out to me because brokenness is what I require.
Then the sound of weeping and crying will be heard no more, and before you call, I will hear.
I will give peace like a river, says the Lord. *To those who are humble in spirit, I will be near.*

Sidebar: Isaiah

REPENTANCE AND REST

> *This is what the Sovereign Lord, the Holy One of Israel, says:*
> *In repentance and rest is your salvation, in quietness and trust is your strength.*
>
> Isaiah 30:15

I can't count how many times I have had my mind made up about something before asking God about it. When I have my mind made up, I am prone to do whatever I want to do regardless of what God says about it. Then I am guilty of disobedience to God.

The process of hearing from God involves approaching God with anticipation, expectation, and patience, and the enthusiasm, desire, and commitment to be obedient. When I know God's Word and I don't obey Him that is sin and rebellion. I can choose to listen and obey God and reap the rewards. Or I can choose to be disobedient and suffer the consequences.

A consequence of disobedience is spiritual famine—the inability to hear God when He speaks. Sometimes disastrous consequences can occur. The rewards for listening to and obeying God include a hunger for His Word and His presence, blessings, rest, peace, righteousness, and the opportunity to be a part of His plan. Imagine what miraculous things we may miss out on when we refuse to be obedient.

Once we have prepared ourselves to hear from God and to be obedient, we must actually listen for God to speak. He speaks to us through prayer, worship, His Word, godly friends, and meditation. We speak to Him through our repentance and prayer. When we take time to rest in Him and meditate, we give the Holy Spirit time to work in us.

According to 1 Corinthians 2:10–12, the Spirit searches all things—our deepest thoughts and God's thoughts. As we meditate, God directs our thoughts, our words, and our attitudes. Through meditation, the Holy Spirit refreshes us, opens our ears and turns our rebellious heart toward Him. Meditation focuses our attention from us and our needs to God and His voice. As we expectantly and patiently wait with anticipation for God to speak, we prepare to be obedient and make time to hear from Him.

GOD REMEMBERS

(Inspired by the book of Isaiah)

When I look back at the early years of my life,
I remember abandonment, abuse, and strife.
I regret the bad choices that I made.
Where are you God? I would pray.

I have been with you from the start.
Your name is written in my heart
and engraved on the palms of my hands.
For you, says the Lord, *I have great plans.*

ISAIAH

Now I see God's hand at work from the beginning,
guiding me, comforting me, watching me, and acting.
He gave me family who made sure I went to church.
In every pain, circumstance, and situation, He heard.

Throughout the Bible, God remembers His people.
At just the right time, He rescues us from evil.
I am so thankful for His love, His grace, and His mercy,
and that He worked everything out for my good and His glory.

CHAPTER EIGHTEEN

JEREMIAH

"For I know the plans I have for you," declares the Lord, "plans to prosper you and not to harm you, plans to give you hope and a future."

Jeremiah 29:11

JEREMIAH THE PROPHET

(Jeremiah Chapters 1–17)

Jeremiah was called to be a prophet from his youth.
He was set apart to tell the kings of Judah the truth.
"I have appointed you," came the word of the Lord.
"I knew you and called you before you were ever born."

Jeremiah replied, "But Lord, I do not know how to speak, and I am too young."
Then God said, "Do not be afraid, go and speak what I put on your tongue. Today I appoint you over nations and kingdoms to uproot and annihilate, to destroy and overthrow, and to build and plant and to create.

"Disaster will fall on my people because of their wickedness,
so stand up and get ready for my words you will profess.
I have made you a fortified city, an iron pillar, and a bronze wall to stand against the kings of Judah, its officials, its priests, and the people of the land.

"They will fight against you, but you will not be overcome,
for I am with you and I will rescue you from them.
Tell my people that this is what the Lord asks, *Why have you strayed so far from me?*
Why have you turned your back on the Lord, and forgotten all my good deeds?

You have exchanged your living God for worthless and dead idols.
Your wickedness will punish you, and your backsliding will bring trials.
You turn from me, then run back to me after you are in trouble.
Where are your man-made gods in the midst of all the rubble?"

Then the Lord said to Jeremiah, "Despite their unfaithfulness, tell them this.
Return to me, declares the Lord, *my people who are so faithless.*
I will not frown on you or be angry forever, my chosen nation.
Return to me and I will heal you, and you will find salvation."

Then Jeremiah said, "Woe to us! We are ruined! These are our consequences.
Wash the evil from your heart and be saved, and come to your senses.
I am in anguish; my heart is pierced and I writhe in pain.
I cannot keep silent. Disaster follows disaster in vain."

You people who have forsaken me for other gods,
the Lord says, will soon worship them on foreign sod.
You foolish people who have eyes but do not see and ears but do not hear.
Tremble in the presence of the Creator for it is me you should fear.

This city is filled with oppression, and as a well pours out its water, it pours out wickedness.
It resounds with violence and destruction, and before me are its wounds and sickness.

JEREMIAH

Your ears are closed, says the Lord, *and my words are offensive to you.*
You are not even ashamed that you practice deceit in all that you do.

Reform your ways, and I will let you live in this place.
Do not trust in deceptive words that people say.
Deal with each other justly, do not oppress orphans, widows, or foreigners,
nor shed innocent blood, follow other gods, or the things that hinder.

I spoke to you again and again, but you did not listen.
I called to you, but you did not answer or pay attention.
You are not just provoking me or dishonoring my name,
you are also harming yourselves, to your own shame.

I told your ancestors, "Keep my covenant and obey my laws,
and you will be my people, and I will be your God."
Then I fulfilled the promise to give them a land flowing with milk and honey.
This is the very land you now possess, if you will only listen to me.

You broke the covenant I made with your ancestors.
Now you are facing certain disaster.
Your gods to whom you burn incense will not save you.
You rejoice in your wickedness and bad behavior.

Jeremiah said, "You are always righteous, Lord.
Yet the wicked prosper and receive rewards.
You are always on their lips but far from their hearts.
But You know me, Lord, and test my thoughts.

"Remember me and care for me, for Your sake.
Although I suffer for You, Your words I ate.
They were my joy and my heart's delight
for I bear Your name both day and night."

This is what the Lord says to His servant,
I will restore you and lift your burden.
I will make you like a wall to these people.
They will not overcome you with their evil.

The person who turns away from God is like a bush in the desert.
They dwell in the parched places in a salt land, alone like a hermit.
But the one who trusts in God is like a tree planted by water.
They do not fear when heat comes, and in drought never falter.

"The heart is deceitful above all, and helpless.
No man can understand it." Jeremiah said.
"Only the Lord can search hearts and examine minds
to reward each person for their deeds in due time.

"The Lord is the hope and strength of His people.
But these people have forsaken You for evil.
Heal me and I will be healed; save me and I will be saved.
You, Lord, are my strength and fortress; the One I praise."

THE FALL OF THE KINGDOM OF JUDAH

(Jeremiah Chapters 18-52)

"Go down to the potter's house," said the Lord.
"There I will give you my important words."
In the potter's hands, the pot was marred;
so he formed it into another one less scarred.

Then the Lord says to Jeremiah, *My people are like clay in my hands.*
I can destroy or I can relent and not follow through on my plans.
Buy a clay pot and break it on the ground, then tell my people,
"This nation will be smashed if they do not repent and turn from evil."

One day the official in charge of the temple heard Jeremiah,
so he had him beaten and put in stocks for his defiance.
Then Jeremiah lamented to the Lord about his woes.
I am ridiculed, but God is with me to defeat my foes.

This is what the Lord says, *I am setting before you death or life.*
Do no wrong, rescue the oppressed, and do what is just and right.

JEREMIAH

The days are coming when, from David's house, a king will rule with favor.
He will be called by this name: The Lord Our Righteous Savior.

My eyes watch over my people for their good.
I will bring them back to where they once stood.
I will give them a heart to know me that I am the Lord.
They will be my people and I will be their God, as before.

For twenty-three years, Jeremiah told the people.
"I have spoken to you again and again about your evil.
Even to all the prophets before me, you have not listened.
Destruction will come because you did not pay attention."

Jeremiah stood in the courtyard and spoke to the crowd.
The people seized him as they became very loud.
"Why do you say these things? You must die!"
they shouted as they began to scream and cry.

The priests and prophets wanted to sentence him to death.
Jeremiah stood his ground, even if it meant his last breath.
Then the officials and all the people had second thoughts.
"This man should not be put to death! He speaks for God."

They knew that Jeremiah spoke the truth and not lies,
so they spared him and decided he did not have to die.
Jeremiah wrote a letter to the exiled remnant—God's people.
He told them not to believe the lies of the prophets of evil.

When the time comes, I will bring my people home.
I will fulfill my promise and you will leave Babylon.
I know what kind of plans I have for you, my people.
They are plans to prosper you and not for evil.

They are plans to give you hope and a future, says God Almighty.
Then you will call on me, seek me, and come and pray to me.
I will listen to you, and you will find me.
I will bring you back from your captivity.

When you seek me with all your heart, I will be found.
I will return you to the land from which I brought you out.
The Lord told Jeremiah to write all these things down in a book.
The Lord said, "Everything will be restored that the enemy took."

I have always loved my people with an everlasting love,
and have drawn them with unfailing kindness from above.
Sing with joy and shout for the nations. Make your praises heard.
I will bring them together and gather them from the ends of the earth.

I will deliver them and redeem them from the hand of their oppressors.
They will come, shout for joy, and rejoice in God's bountiful treasures.
They will be like a well-watered garden and no longer be sad.
I will turn their mourning into joy; they will dance and be glad.

The days are coming when I will make a covenant with you.
It will not be like the old covenant of your ancestors, but new.
I will put my law in your minds and write it on your hearts.
You will know me; I will forgive and give you a fresh start.

King Zedekiah had Jeremiah imprisoned in the courtyard.
While he was confined there, he heard these words of the Lord.
I am the Lord, God of everything, and nothing is too hard for me.
I will never stop doing good for my people in their time of need.

Call to me and I will answer and tell you unsearchable things.
Though tragedy comes, I will heal my people and bring them peace.
I will bring them back from captivity and rebuild their cities.
I will prosper them and cleanse them from their iniquity.

"Take a scroll and write down every one of these words.
Perhaps my people will turn back to me," said the Lord.
Jeremiah sent his friend Baruch to read the scroll to the people
since Jeremiah was not allowed to go to the Lord's temple.

The king sent one of his men to retrieve the scroll,
but he did not like the things that it foretold.

JEREMIAH

So he cut up the scroll, and tossed it into the firepot to burn.
He tried to arrest the men of God, but the Lord had hid them.

Jeremiah wrote another scroll as the Lord had directed,
and for the king's wickedness, disaster was predicted.
Jeremiah had been imprisoned in a dungeon and then a courtyard.
Now the king had Jeremiah arrested and put into a cistern full of mud.

Once the king realized that he had acted wickedly,
he had Jeremiah removed from the cistern immediately.
Jeremiah was placed back in the courtyard, under arrest.
He remained there until Jerusalem was taken and oppressed.

Nebuchadnezzar, king of Babylon, marched against the city.
His army laid siege and broke through the walls quickly.
The Babylonians set fire to the royal palace and the houses,
and they carried the people off into exile by the masses.

King Nebuchadnezzar gave orders not to harm the prophet.
He had found Jeremiah bound in chains among the captives.
He told Jeremiah to go anywhere he wanted to go.
Jeremiah chose to remain among his people though.

Some of the remnant approached Jeremiah and asked him,
"Please pray to God that He will tell us what to do again."
"I have heard you," replied Jeremiah, "and this is what the Lord says,
Stay in this land and do not fear the king for I know what is best.

I will build you up, not tear you down, if you stay in this land.
I am with you and will save you and deliver you from his hands.
I will show compassion on you and restore you to your land."
But the people doubted and would not believe God's command.

They entered Egypt in disobedience to God Almighty.
Then king Nebuchadnezzar attacked and conquered the country.
"I will repay the evil done against my people," God gave this assurance.
"You will be avenged; come out of Babylon and find deliverance."

Nebuchadnezzar took all the things King Solomon had made for the temple.
In all of the exiles taken away, there were four thousand six hundred people.
Jeremiah carried the Lord's message to the people for over forty years.
His ministry spanned the reigns of five kings and many tears.

I KNOW THE PLANS

(Inspired by the book of Jeremiah)

"Before I created you, I knew you," said the Lord.
"I set you apart even before you were born.
I remember the love you had for me
when you were as innocent as a baby.

"What have I done to make you run away?
You chose selfish ambition and went astray.
You forsook me, and dug your own grave.
Your own wickedness will make you a slave.

"You have rebelled against me and been disobedient.
Return to me, faithless child, and find atonement.
Acknowledge your guilt and I will not be angry.
I am faithful and I want you to return to me."

"I have sinned against You," I said. "My Lord and my God,
my disgrace covers me; I am full of shame and flawed.
I went my own way and continued my misbehavior;
but I will come to You for You are my Lord and Savior."

"Stand at the crossroads and look; ask where the good way is.
Seek me and you will find rest for your soul if you walk in it.
Walk in obedience to all that I command you," said the Lord.
"I have wept day and night for my people that I adore.

"I know what plans I have for you, plans to prosper you,
not to harm you, but to give you hope and a future too.

JEREMIAH

Call on me and come and pray to me, and I will listen.
You will seek me with all of your heart and attention.

"I will be found by you, and I will bring you back from captivity.
I will break your chains and sever your bonds," said God Almighty.
"I have always loved you with an everlasting love,
and drawn you with unfailing kindness from above.

"Sing and shout for joy, and make your praises heard.
I will deliver you and redeem you according to my word.
I will turn your mourning into gladness
and give you comfort instead of sadness.

"My heart yearns for you with compassion," said the Lord.
"I will put my law in your mind and write it on your heart.
I will forgive your wickedness and forgive your sins too.
Only if the Heavens could be measured, would I reject you."

You are my sovereign Lord who created the Heavens and earth.
Nothing is too hard for You; great are Your deeds and Your worth.
I repented after I understood the disgrace of my past and youth,
I prayed. *You discipline me and restore me, and I will return to You.*

CHAPTER NINETEEN

LAMENTATIONS

Let us examine our ways and test them, and let us return to the Lord.

Lamentations 3:40

THE LAMENTATIONS OF JEREMIAH

(Lamentations Chapters 1–5)

These are the lamentations of Jeremiah after the fall of Jerusalem:
Where there once was a city full of people, now captivity has come.
She was once queen among the cities, but is now a slave.
The bitter tears that she cries at night stain her face.

She has no comfort or rest from her affliction.
She grieves in bitter anguish at her desolation.
She has sinned and those who once honored her now despise her.
She remembers the days of old when she was full of God's treasure.

Her enemies look and laugh at her destruction.
Her fall was as astounding as her seduction.
She cannot even look at herself in the mirror,
nor did she ever stop to consider her future.

"As I weep, my eyes overflow with tears."
Said Jeremiah, "There is no comfort; no one is near.
There is no one to comfort me or to restore my spirit.
The enemy has prevailed; my destitute children bear it.

The Lord is righteous, yet I rebelled against his command.
I am in torment and disturbed; see how distressed I am!
We have been rebellious to You, and inside I feel only death.
We have forgotten You, and been ungrateful with every breath.

The walls of Judah's palaces have fallen into the hands of the enemy.
Her king and her princes are exiled among the nations, helplessly.
Her prophets no longer hear from the Lord.
Her elders sit on the ground without a word.

Your false prophets told you worthless lies.
They did not point out the sin that led to your demise.
The hearts of the people cry out for the Lord to save.
There is no relief; their tears flow night and day.

I remember the bitterness of my affliction and wandering.
My soul is downcast within me at my pondering.
Yet I have hope as I call to mind God's great love for us.
We are not devoured because His love never gives up.

The Lord's compassions are new every morning.
I will faithfully wait on Him for He is my portion.
The Lord is good to those who put their hope in Him,
and to those who seek Him and wait for salvation.

Though grief comes, God will show compassion
because of the unfailing love He has for us.

LAMENTATIONS

Let us examine our hearts and test our ways.
Let us return to the Lord and give Him praise.

We lift our hands to You and say, 'We have sinned and rebelled.'
We have suffered destruction, and lost what our hands once held.
You, Lord, remember our sin and see our disgrace.
Still, You redeem us and show us Your face."

CHAPTER TWENTY

EZEKIEL

He said to me, "Son of man, go now to the house of Israel and speak my words to them."

Ezekiel 3:4

THE WATCHMAN

(Ezekiel Chapters 1–36)

These are the words of the prophet Ezekiel,
Spoken (when he was thirty years old) to the people:
As I was with the exiles, the Heavens opened to me.
I saw visions of God and, from the north, a windstorm coming.

There was a huge cloud that flashed with fire and lightning.
There were four heavenly beings inside; their appearance was frightening.
There were four wheels inside: wheels that moved with them.
There was a sky above their heads that sparkled like gems.

When the creatures moved, their wings sounded like rushing water,
like the clamor of an army, or the voice of God the Father.
Then a voice came from a glorious throne made of precious stone.
On it sat a figure like a man, and around Him the glory of God shone.

The radiance around Him was like a rainbow in the clouds on a rainy day.
When I saw it and heard the voice, I fell facedown and heard Him say,
Son of man, stand up and listen—to you I will speak.
I am sending you to my people who have rebelled against me.

They are a stubborn and obstinate people.
They will not repent and turn from their evil.
Do not be afraid of them or anything they say.
But speak my words so they will change their ways.

Then He handed me a scroll and unrolled it before me.
On both sides were written words of woe and mourning.
Then He said, "Son of man, eat this scroll, then carry my words out."
So I ate the scroll, and it tasted like honey in my mouth.

"These people do not want to listen to you because they do not want to listen to me,"
He said. "Because my people are rebellious, obstinate, and unyielding,
I will make you as stubborn and unyielding as they are.
I will make you strong and make your forehead hard."

God gave me specific instructions to pray and intercede.
He told me what to do, how to lay, and what to eat.
He told me to shave my head and beard,
and to use the pieces to make them hear.

Then the Lord said, "These are my people who I have set apart,
but they have rebelled and have wickedness in their hearts.
These people will suffer the consequences of their sin.
They will suffer and be scattered like the wind.

EZEKIEL

"The altars of your idols will be demolished and smashed.
Those who are taken captive will remember who I am.
Their hearts will grieve for the sins they have committed.
Cry out to them for their wickedness habituated.

"The counsel of the elders will come to an end.
The king will mourn; the prince be condemned.
The hands of the people of the land will tremble.
By their own standards, they will be accountable."

Again, the voice of the Sovereign Lord came to me.
He lifted me up and took me to Jerusalem to see.
I saw the detestable things that the people were doing.
They thought God could not see them in their loathing.

God spoke to me about false prophets leading people astray.
They whitewashed the truth with their shades of gray.
They will be punished for their false words
and for leading people away from the Lord.

"I will recapture the hearts of my people
even though they have left me to do evil.
Turn away from your idols," said the Sovereign Lord,
"Repent! I will answer when you listen to my words."

Then God continued, "You will become an example and a byword.
You will come back to me, and you will know that I am the Lord."
"You will be my people, and I will be your God" declared the Sovereign Lord.
"I will restore you. I the Lord have spoken, and these are my words."

God said, "No longer will a child share the guilt of the parent,
nor will the parent share the guilt of the child inherent.
The righteousness of the righteous will be credited to them,
and the wickedness of the wicked will be charged as sin.

"Someday I will bring you out, and I will gather you together.
I will be proven holy when I draw you from where you were scattered.
You will know I am God when I deal with you with mercy
instead of dealing with you and your sin the way it should be.

"Now the king of Babylon has laid siege to the city.
I will not hold back or relent, and I will not have pity.
I have made you Ezekiel, a watchman for the people.
Hear the words I speak and warn them about the evil."

God said to me, "Son of man, prophesy against the leaders.
Although I have trusted them to be the shepherds of my people,
they neglect the sheep, take care of themselves, and get fat from the plunder.
I will hold them accountable and rescue my sheep who will no longer wander.

"My flock will no longer be lost because I will search for and find them.
I will bring them into their own land where they will find a safe haven.
I will bandage the injured and give strength to the weak.
I will lead them to good pasture, and fresh water from the creek.

"I the Lord have spoken. I will save my flock.
They will be my people, and I will be their God.
I will wash them clean and give them a new spirit of refreshing.
I will pour out my Spirit and rain down showers of blessings."

THE RESTORATION OF GOD'S PEOPLE

(Ezekiel Chapters 37–48)

The Lord brought me out to a valley nearby.
It was full of bones that were old and dry.
He asked me, "Son of man, can these bones live?"
I answered, "Only You know; life is Yours to give."

Then God said to me, "Prophesy to these bones and say,
'Dry bones hear the word of the Lord! I will bring you to life today.'"

EZEKIEL

So I prophesied to the old bones—dried up and withered.
As I did, I heard a rattling sound as the bones came together.

Tendons appeared and they were covered with skin,
but still there was no breath in them.
Then God said to me, "Prophesy to the breath and say,
'Come from the four winds and breathe into these slain where they lay.'"

Again I did as God commanded me, and breath entered them.
They came to life and stood up as a great army before Him.
Then He told me that the bones were His children—
that He would open their graves and free them.

"I will bring you back to your land, and you will know that I am the Lord.
Then you will know that I, the Lord, have spoken, and these are my words.
I will put my sanctuary among them forever," the Lord told me.
"Then all the nations will know that I have made my people holy."

In one final vision, God took me to the land of His people.
He set me on a mountain and showed me the new temple.
God blessed His people and covered their sin,
and the glory of God dwelled among them.

BREATHE ON MY DRY BONES

(Inspired by the book of Ezekiel)

I am weak and weary, and my bones are dry.
I thirst for more but am never satisfied.
My soul aches—I know there is something better.
I long for freedom and to be unfettered.

God took my hand and then He said,
"Do you believe I can raise the dead?"
"I believe You can," I replied.
"Help my unbelief to subside."

"Trust me, my child, and take my Hand.
Be still and know that I am who I am."
In the quiet, a rattling sound was heard
as He breathed life and my spirit stirred.

Then my grave was opened, and I saw light.
He defeated the darkness, death, and night.
He reached down and grabbed my hand,
then He put my feet down on dry land.

My hope is gone no longer,
and my faith is made stronger.
I am alive again—His spirit lives in me.
I am His and He is mine for eternity.

Sidebar: Ezekiel

OUR DAILY BREAD

And he said to me, "Son of man, eat what is before you, eat this scroll; then go and speak to the people of Israel." So I opened my mouth, and he gave me the scroll to eat.

Then he said to me, "Son of man, eat this scroll I am giving you and fill your stomach with it." So I ate it, and it tasted as sweet as honey in my mouth.

He then said to me: "Son of man, go now to the people of Israel and speak my words to them."

Ezekiel 3:1–4

Many live as enemies of the cross of Christ. Their destiny is destruction, their god is their stomach, and their glory is in their shame. Their mind is set on earthly things.

Philippians 3:18b–19

We call God's Word our "Daily Bread," but most of us don't even "eat it" once a day. We fill the hole in our stomachs at least three times a day with food. If we would fill the hole in our hearts with God's Word at least once a day, then we wouldn't try to fill it with physical pleasures and earthly desires. Those things are fleeting. Only what is done for the Kingdom will last. We cannot live productive, victorious Christian lives without a constant, consistent diet of God's Word.

When we consistently consume the God-breathed Words of the Bible, it teaches us, rebukes us, corrects us, trains us and it thoroughly equips us for every good work. God's Word is filled with love, redemption, blessing, and promise. God's Word is sweet as honey in our mouths. God's Word is not just a roadmap. It is life.

When we feel used and abused, the Bible says we are loved.

When we feel abandoned, the Bible says we are never alone.

When we feel rejected, the Bible says we are redeemed.

When we feel lost, the Bible is a lamp for our feet and a light on our path.

When we feel worthless, the Bible says that we are God's handiwork created in Christ Jesus to do good works, which He prepared in advance for us to do.

When Satan tries to trick us into believing that we belong to the darkness, the Bible says that we are children of the light and children of the day; that we do not belong to the night or to the darkness.

When we need direction, the Bible says that God will make us worthy of His calling. The Bible tells us that by God's power He will bring to fruition our every desire for goodness and our every deed prompted by faith. All of this is so that the name of Jesus may be glorified in us, and us in Him, according to His grace.

We should be so thankful for God's Word that we never lose the desire to devour it.[2]

---

2. Psalm 119:105; Ephesians 2:10; 1 Thessalonians 5:5; 2; Thessalonians 1:11–12

CHAPTER TWENTY-ONE

DANIEL

If we are thrown into the blazing furnace, the God we serve is able to deliver us from it, ...But even if he does not, ...we will not serve your gods or worship the image of gold you have set up.

Daniel 3:17–18

THE FIERY FURNACE

(Daniel Chapters 1–4)

Nebuchadnezzar was the king of Babylon.
He besieged and conquered Jerusalem.
He carried away some of the articles from God's temple
and put them in the treasure house of his own idol.

The king ordered that young men be brought to the palace—
handsome men that were well learned and full of valor.
He asked for the men to be from Israel's royals and nobility
and that they possess aptitude, understanding, and ability.

He brought the men to Babylon to serve the king's court.
They were to learn the language, the literature, and the art.
The men were assigned a daily amount of food and wine.
They were to enter the king's service after three years' time.

Hananiah, Mishael, Azariah, and Daniel were the names of the men.
The chief official changed their names from what they had been.
Daniel became Belteshazzar; Hananiah became Shadrach;
Azariah became Abednego; and Mishael became Meshach.

Daniel did not want to eat the royal food and be defiled,
so he asked to not partake in the things that are reviled.
Daniel said, "Give us nothing but vegetables to eat and water to drink.
After ten days, compare us with the others and see what you think."

The chief official agreed and tested them for ten days.
Daniel and his friends looked healthier, and the chief was amazed.
God gave these young men knowledge and wisdom.
Daniel could understand all types of dreams and visions.

The young men were presented to King Nebuchadnezzar.
He found no equals in the land—none whatsoever.
The king had troubling dreams that kept him awake at night.
His wise men could not interpret them, try as they might.

Daniel came before the king and asked for time to contemplate.
Then he went to his friends and asked them to pray and wait.
During the night, the dream was revealed in a vision.
So he praised God for His great power and wisdom.

Daniel went before the king and said, "No wise man can explain your dream,
but there is a God in Heaven who reveals mysteries and knows everything."
Then Daniel told the king not only what he dreamed but also what it meant.
The king fell down before Daniel and said, "Great is the God you represent."

DANIEL

Then the king elevated Daniel to a high position
and made his friends administrators in addition.
The king made an image of gold ninety feet high and nine feet wide.
He summoned all the important people of the land to his side.

As the people stood before the image for the dedication,
the herald proclaimed, "This is the king's proclamation:
When you hear the instruments play and the horns blow,
fall down and worship the image of gold and bow low.

"Anyone who does not worship will be thrown into a blazing furnace."
As the music played, everyone bowed except God's servants.
Shadrach, Meshach, and Abednego refused to worship.
The king had them brought before him as insurgents.

He said, "If you do not bow, then you will burn."
They answered, "We trust in the God we serve.
If we are thrown into the furnace, our God can save us.
But even if he does not, we will not waiver."

Then Nebuchadnezzar was furious with them, and his attitude changed.
He had the men make the furnace seven times hotter than the usual flames.
The fire was so hot that it killed the soldiers holding the men,
as they carried the three, clothed and bound, and threw them in.

The king jumped up in amazement and exclaimed,
"Weren't there three men thrown into the flames?
Look! There are four men walking around.
They are unharmed and unbound.

"The fourth man in the furnace looks like a son of God.
Come out, Shadrach, Meshach, and Abednego," the king said, awed.
As the crowds gathered around the men,
they saw that not a hair on their heads was singed.

Their clothes were not burnt, and the fire had done them no harm.
There was no smell of fire and the ropes were removed from their arms.
"These men were willing to die rather than worship an idol.
Praise be to their God," the king said. "He is faithful."

Then the king proceeded to promote the three men,
and told the people everything that happened to him.
He said, "Glorify the King of Heaven because everything he does is right.
His ways are just, and he humbles those who walk in pride."

THE LION'S DEN

(Daniel Chapters 5–12)

Nebuchadnezzar's son, Belshazzar, gave a great banquet.
As they drank wine, he sent for the objects from the temple theft.
They brought in the stolen objects and drank from the goblets of gold,
as they praised the gods of gold, silver, bronze, iron, wood, and stone.

Suddenly the fingers of a human hand appeared and wrote on the wall.
The king was so terrified that his knees became weak, and he began to fall.
He called his astrologers and diviners to translate what was written.
But they could not understand: the meaning was still hidden.

"May the king live forever. Don't be alarmed!" said the queen.
"There is a man named Daniel who interpreted your father's dreams.
With wisdom, knowledge, and insight, he has been blessed.
Call for him and he can tell you what the writing says."

The king called for Daniel and brought him before the court.
"I will tell you what the writing says," came Daniel's retort.
"Your father Nebuchadnezzar humbled himself before the Most High.
But you have not honored the God who holds in His hand your life.

"This is what the inscription that was written means:
God has numbered your days of being king.

DANIEL

You have been weighed on the scales and found wanting.
Your kingdom will be taken, and a new day is dawning."

Daniel was made the third highest ruler in the kingdom,
as a reward from the king for his honesty and wisdom.
That same night, King Belshazzar was slain,
and Darius the Mede began his reign.

Daniel's exceptional qualities gave him favor with the new king.
The other administrators were jealous, and they began to scheme.
They could find no grounds for charges against Daniel,
so they deceived the king into making a new rule.

They said, "We all agree that people should only pray to you,
so sign a decree that for thirty days that is all they can do.
Anyone who prays to any other god should be thrown into the lion's den."
So the king signed the decree that everyone should pray only to him.

When Daniel learned about the decree, he went home to pray,
just as he had done before, three times a day.
Then the men went before the king and said,
"Daniel pays no attention to the decree that was read."

The king was greatly distressed and tried to save Daniel.
But the men reminded him that he could not change the rule.
So they threw Daniel into the lion's den and placed a stone over the mouth too.
The king said to Daniel, "May your God, whom you serve continually, rescue you!"

The king did not eat or sleep all night.
He ran to the lion's den at first light.
He called out to Daniel in anguish and grief.
Daniel answered, "My God saved me, O King.

"An angel came and shut the lion's mouth.
I was found innocent by God and devout."

The king gave orders to bring Daniel out of the den.
There was not a wound, mark, or scratch on him.

Then the king issued a decree that all must exalt the true God.
"He is the living God and He endures forever; give Him laud.
He rescues and He saves and He performs signs and wonders,
on the earth and in the Heavens with lightning and thunder."

Throughout the reigns of kings, Daniel had dreams and visions.
He saw what was going to happen to the people because of their decisions.
He saw visions of the end times and visions of the future.
He pleaded, prayed, and fasted about what was to occur.

"Lord, the great and awesome God," he prayed and confessed.
"To those who love and honor You, You keep Your covenant.
We have sinned and done wrong, been wicked, and rebelled.
We have turned away from You, and Your laws we have not upheld.

"We have not listened to Your servants, the prophets.
Lord, You are merciful, forgiving, and righteous.
Because of our unfaithfulness, we are covered with shame.
We have brought disaster upon ourselves, but still will not call Your name.

"We have not payed attention to the truth nor sought Your favor.
But You, Lord our God, are righteous in everything—You are our Savior.
Hear and answer us, not because of our righteousness,
but because of Your great deeds, Your mercy, and Your forgiveness."

As Daniel was again praying and seeking the Lord,
he had another vision concerning a great war.
"At the end of this, many will be purified, refined, and made spotless,"
the Lord said, "but you will rest and receive your allotted inheritance."

SECTION FOUR

The Minor Prophets

CHAPTER TWENTY-TWO

HOSEA

"I led them with cords of human kindness, with ties of love. To them I was like one who lifts a little child to the cheek, and I bent down to feed them." (God)

Hosea 11:4

GOD'S FAITHFUL LOVE

(Hosea Chapters 1–14)

The Lord told Hosea, "Go and marry a prostitute,
and other men's children will be born to you.
This will be an illustration of how my people have strayed,
and how my love for them will always remain the same."

Hosea married a woman named Gomer, and she had children.
He named them according to what the Lord had spoken.
Their names illustrated the actions of God's people
and how they had turned away from Him to evil.

"Yet I will show love to them and save them," said the Lord,
"not by bow or battle, or by horses and horsemen, or by sword.
They are not acting like my children at this present time.
Yet they will be like the sand on the seashore, these people of Mine.

"Their number cannot be counted or measured.
They will be my people and my treasure.
But they are like a prostitute, going wherever their desires lead.
I will block their path, and then they will come back to me.

"I will court them again and speak tenderly.
They will sing with joy in response to me.
I will make them forget their idols, and their names will not be spoken.
I will bind them to me with chains of mercy that will not be broken."

The Lord said to Hosea, "Go, show your love to your wife again,
even though she is an adulteress and loved by other men.
Love her as the Lord loves His people, though they turn to their idols.
They do not acknowledge or love their God and have been unfaithful.

"The people will say, 'Come, let us return to the Lord.
He has torn us to pieces, but He will restore.
He has injured us, but He will bind up our wounds and heal us.
He will come and revive us that we may live in his presence.'"

"I desire mercy, not sacrifice, and gratitude rather than burnt offerings.
I desire justice and redemption over destruction and posturing.
Sow righteousness for yourselves, reap the fruit of unfailing love,
and break up your unplowed ground—it is time to seek God above.

"With cords of human kindness, with ties of love, I led my people.
But they are determined to turn away from me, and determined to seek evil.
Still my heart is full of compassion for them.
I will not devastate them for their sin.

HOSEA

"For I am God, and not a man— the Holy One among you.
But you must return to me, maintain love, and to justice be true.
I have been the Lord your God ever since you came out of Egypt.
You shall acknowledge no other Savior but me—all others reject.

"I cared for you in the wilderness, in the land of burning heat.
When I fed you, you were satisfied, then became proud and forgot me.
Return, people, to the Lord your God who led you faithfully.
Say to Him, 'Forgive all our sins and receive us graciously.

"'We will never again say "our gods" to what our hands have made.
For in You, the fatherless find compassion and the lost find their way.'
I will heal their waywardness and love them freely,
for my anger has turned away from them completely.

"My people will be blessed, will flourish and prosper.
I will answer and take care of them like their Father.
My ways are right, and the righteous walk in them,
but the rebellious will stumble around in their sin."

CHAPTER TWENTY-THREE

JOEL

*"And afterward, I will pour out my Spirit on all people.
Your sons and daughters will prophesy, your old men will
dream dreams, your young men will see visions." (God).*

Joel 2:28

WHAT THE LOCUSTS HAVE DESTROYED

(Joel Chapters 1–3)

This is what the Lord says to Joel the prophet:
"Listen to me as I tell of things to come that are catastrophic.
Nothing like what I am about to say has ever happened in your time.
Tell this to every generation, and keep it on their minds.

"Wake up, you drunkards, and see that your wine is gone.
Everything has been devoured by the locusts' swarm.
Grain and drink offerings are cut off from the house of the Lord.
The priests are in mourning, those who minister God's word.

"Give up hope, you growers and farmers of the field.
The harvest is destroyed; there is no more yield.
Mourn and wail, you people, as your joy withers away.
The vines and the trees have dried up and decayed.

"Declare a holy fast, and call a sacred assembly.
Summon everyone to the house of the Lord to meet humbly.
Cry out to God because the day of destruction is near.
Cry out to the Lord your God in reverence and fear.

"The day of the Lord is great and dreadful. Who can endure it?
Return to God with all your heart, with fasting, mourning, and tenderness.
Return to the Lord your God for he is gracious and compassionate,
slow to anger, and abounding in love and affectionate."

Then the Lord was protective for His land and took pity on His people.
The Lord replied to them, *"I will take care of you and deliver you from evil.*
I will give back to you all that the locusts have destroyed.
You will eat until you are full and praise my name and rejoice.

"Then you will know that I am the Lord your God, and there is no other.
I will pour out my Spirit on all people and show signs and wonders.
And everyone who calls on the name of the Lord will be saved;
there will be deliverance, and the name of the Lord will be praised.

"I will restore my people and gather them together.
They will see justice done to their oppressors.
I will be a refuge and stronghold for my children.
They will know that I, the Lord God, dwell in them."

CHAPTER TWENTY-FOUR

AMOS

And the Lord asked me, "What do you see, Amos?" "A plumb line," I replied. Then the Lord said, "Look, I am setting a plumb line among my people Israel; I will spare them no longer."

Amos 7:8

FROM SHEPHERD TO PROPHET

(Amos Chapters 1–9)

These are the words of the prophet Amos, who was a shepherd.
Amos had a vision concerning Israel, and this is the record.
The Lord roars from Zion and thunders from Jerusalem;
the pastures of the shepherds dry up and are of no use to them.

For these people who have sinned over and over again,
justice will come, and I, the Lord, will not relent.
I brought you up out of Egypt and led you forty years.
I brought you through the wilderness through trials and tears.

Even though I gave you everything, you still were not satisfied.
You did not listen, and commanded the prophets not to prophesy.
Hear this word of the Lord that is spoken against you,
I have chosen only you and to You I have been true.

I have remained true to you, says the Lord.
But you still choose to despise my word.
I have tried to beckon you back to me again and again.
Soon the time will come when you will pay for your sins.

He is the Lord, the one who forms mountains and tells the wind to blow.
He turns dawn to darkness and makes the sun and moon glow.
He reveals his thoughts for mankind to proclaim,
because the Lord God Almighty is his name.

This is what the Lord God says, *Seek me and live.*
There are those who turn justice into bitterness and do not forgive.
He who calls for the waters of the sea and pours them out over the land—
The Lord is His name. He is the Holy One of Israel, the Great I Am.

Hate evil, love good, and maintain justice.
Perhaps the Lord will have mercy on us.
Let justice flow like a river, and righteousness like a stream!
Instead you lift up the shrine of your idols and your kings.

Woe to you who are complacent and to you who feel secure.
You indulge in sin, but you do not grieve over the ruin of the pure.
You will be the first to go into exile; your feasting and lounging will end.
You have turned justice into poison and righteousness into bitter sin.

The Lord was standing by a wall that had been built straight and true.
With a plumb line in his hand, He asked me, "What do you see before you?"
"A plumb line," I replied. Then the Lord said, "My people will be tested.
I am disappointed in them and with a plumb line they will be measured."

Amaziah the priest of Bethel conspired against Amos.
The priest stated claims to the king that were heinous.

He told the king that Amos was speaking against him.
He stirred up lies and told Amos to leave the kingdom.

Amos answered, "I was not a prophet but a shepherd.
But then the Lord sent me to prophesy to His treasure.
*You will suffer the consequences of your sin and your lies.
And God's treasure—His people—will be carried off into exile.*

"God has had enough of your sin and debauchery;
of those who rob the poor and trample the needy;
of those crooks who ask, 'When will we get paid again?'
Then you cheat people and take advantage of them."

The Lord says, *I will never forget what they have done.
The land will tremble and the people will mourn as one.
The days are coming when I will send famine through the land—
not for food and water, but for the words of the Lord to man.*

I saw the Lord standing by the altar, and he said to me,
"My people will suffer and there will be nowhere to flee.
But the time will come when I will replant this nation.
Never again will they be uprooted from their foundation."

Sidebar: Amos

TRUTH, LIES, AND A PLUMB LINE

A plumb line is a cord or string with a weight on one end that is used to determine verticality. It was used to make sure a wall was straight and true. God uses a plumb line to measure how straight and true we stand.

In Isaiah 28, the Lord says, "I will make justice the measuring line and righteousness the plumb line." God measures His people by how we show justice and mercy to others, and by how we walk righteously with Him. He requires us to seek justice, love mercy, and to walk humbly with Him (Micah 6:8). In the book of Amos, the Lord stood by a wall that had been built straight to a plumb line and said to Amos, "Look, I am setting a plumb line among my people Israel." God had shown mercy over and over again to His people. Now it was time to stop overlooking their sin. It was time for the people to begin living up to His standards.

God has set standards of behavior for us. He has set a plumb line for us. His Word is our plumb line, and we should measure ourselves by that line. He will only tolerate our wickedness for so long. It is time to fall down on our knees in repentance and prayer, to stand up with Him and speak out to the world.

We will not be measured by the world's standards anymore. We will be measured by the plumb line of God's Word. We will be people who live out our Christianity by walking faithfully in obedience to God. We will love mercy and justice. We will love others the way God loves us—unconditionally, relentlessly, and with grace.

CHAPTER TWENTY-FIVE

OBADIAH

The day of the Lord is near for all nations. As you have done, it will be done to you; your deeds will return upon your own head.

Obadiah 1:15

A FIRE AND A FLAME

(Obadiah Chapter 1)

God gave Obadiah a vision about the future of His nation.
An envoy came with a report from the Lord for the evil generation.
God says, *I will cut you down to size.*
Among the nations, you will be small and despised.

You think you are inaccessible living way up high.
You have been deceived by your evil heart that is full of pride.
Do not be fooled thinking you will never be brought down.
Though you soar among the stars, you will plummet to the ground.

Your allies will turn against you to force you out.
They will promise peace but lies are what they spout.
Your friends will deceive you and try to set traps.
Your mightiest soldiers will be terrified of mishaps.

All these things will happen because of your sin.
You will be exposed and ashamed for what has been.
You deserted your family in their time of need.
As you have done, you will be repaid deed for deed.

Some will escape to a place where they will be safe.
They will become conquerors, a fire, and a flame.
They will reoccupy the land and return to their home,
and the kingdom they establish will belong to the Lord alone.

CHAPTER TWENTY-SIX

JONAH

But Jonah ran away from the Lord and headed for Tarshish. He went down to Joppa, where he found a ship bound for that port. After paying the fare, he went aboard and sailed for Tarshish to flee from the Lord.

Jonah 1:3

A FISH CALLED GRACE

(Jonah Chapters 1–4)

God told Jonah the prophet to go to Nineveh,
"Go and preach to them about their wickedness."
Jonah did not like the people, so he headed to Tarshish.
He went down to Joppa where he boarded a ship.

Then the Lord sent a great wind on the ocean,
so violently that it shook the ship with its motion.
All the sailors were afraid and cried out to their gods.
Then they began throwing all the cargo overboard.

Jonah was below the deck of the ship sleeping.
The captain ran down to Jonah pleading,
"Wake up and call on your God to help us.
Maybe He will save us, and we will not perish."

Then the sailors drew straws to see who was responsible.
Jonah drew the short straw which was inevitable.
The sailors asked him, "Who are you and where are you from?"
He answered, "I am a prophet. From the God of Heaven, I come."

The men were terrified and asked Jonah, "What have you done?"
"I disobeyed God," he answered, "and I tried to run.
Throw me overboard and the storm will cease."
So they threw him out, and there was peace.

God provided a big fish that swallowed Jonah on sight,
and he was in its belly for three days and three nights.
From inside the fish, Jonah prayed to the Lord and said
"In my distress, I called You, Lord, from the realm of the dead.

"You answered me when I called for help and listened to me.
You hurled me into the depths, the very heart of the sea.
The waters engulfed me and seaweed wrapped around my head.
But you, Lord my God, brought my life up from the dead.

"Now, with shouts of grateful praise, I will share Your words.
I will say to the people, 'Salvation comes from the Lord.'"
Then the Lord commanded the fish to vomit Jonah out,
so the fish threw him up on the shore to preach aloud.

This time Jonah listened to the Lord and obeyed.
He preached to the entire city for three days.
The Ninevites believed God, and they repented.
Then God had compassion on them and relented.

But Jonah was angry and did not agree with God's decision.
He said, "I knew that You are full of grace and compassion,

abounding in love and slow to anger,
and You would relent from sending danger.

"I would rather die right now than live in my misery."
Then God said, "Is it right for you to be angry?"
Jonah went out, made a shelter, and sat in the shade.
Then he sat under a leafy plant that God had made.

Jonah was happy until a worm came and ate the leaves.
Then the sun blazed, and he grew faint and sought death for relief.
"Is it right for you to be angry?" God asked again.
"I am so angry; I wish I could die," Jonah said.

"You were concerned about this plant although you did not create it.
It sprang up overnight," God said, "and died as I permitted.
But you think I should not have saved these people
from death, destruction, and evil."

Sidebar: Jonah

OVERCOMING PREJUDICE

Almost everyone knows the story of Jonah and the Whale. Jonah did not like the Ninevites because of the way they had mistreated the Israelites. So when God sent Jonah to preach the message of salvation to the people of Nineveh, Jonah ran. He didn't run because he was afraid. He ran because he was prejudiced against the Ninevites. He hated them so much that he wanted them to burn in hell.

I am the type of person that likes most people. I consider myself to be an unprejudiced person. But that doesn't mean that prejudice and hatred don't sometimes creep out of my sinful nature. I sometimes find myself being prejudiced against certain types of people because of my past. When I don't look at others through the eyes of God's love, I find myself judging others (sometimes for the very sins that God saved me from).

Jonah repented for his sins and went back to Nineveh. (Well actually, he repented and agreed to God's will, then the fish threw him up on the shores of Nineveh). Jonah preached the gospel of sin and the gospel of God's love and salvation to the people, and they turned from their sin. Can you imagine such a joyous day? A whole city turned to God!

Yet because of bitterness and hatred, Jonah refused to be happy that God had used him for such an amazing purpose. Instead he was angry and pouted. Jonah felt wronged that God would save the Ninevites after everything they had done. He was so angry at the compassion and grace of God that he wanted to die. He prayed to the Lord,

> *Isn't this what I said, Lord, when I was still at home? That is what I tried to forestall by fleeing to Tarshish. I knew that you are a gracious and compassionate God, slow to anger and abounding in love, a God who relents from sending calamity. Now, Lord, take away my life, for it is better for me to die than to live.*
>
> *Jonah 4:2–3*

I remember the funeral of the uncle who abused me and took away my innocence. I was almost a little sad that I had never faced him to say that I forgave him for what he had done and that what the devil intended for bad, God had worked out for His glory and my good. At the funeral when I found out that He had found salvation, I was furious. Feelings of anger, resentment, and yes even hatred that I thought I had dealt with came flooding in. I was angry that my uncle was not going to burn in hell for what he had done to me. I was angry at God that He would "dare" forgive someone like my uncle.

Then just like God's response in Jonah 4:4, I heard His words: "Is it right for you to be angry?" No! It wasn't right! I had no right to judge anyone! Who was I to put boundaries on God's forgiveness? If God had put boundaries on His grace and mercy to me, when would enough have been enough? After the first relapse? After the second or third time I turned my back and ran from Him? After I put people I love in harm's way because I couldn't say no? After the tenth or fifteenth time I drove drunk? After the thousandth time I questioned Him or told Him I didn't want or need His help? Where would I be if God had placed boundaries on His love for me?

I shouldn't have so little control over myself or my reverence for God that I become displeased or angry with God when He practices His true nature. If we are truly disciples of Christ, then whatever pleases God should please us. And what pleases God is that no one should perish, "but everyone should come to repentance" (2 Peter 3:9).

I shouldn't complain about God's mercy to others while thanking Him for His mercy to me. I shouldn't commit the sin of pride by justifying my rebellion or my running from God compared to other people's sin.

Who am I to be angry at what the angels in Heaven rejoice in? Matthew Henry says it beautifully:

> *"We do ill to be angry at that grace which we ourselves need and are undone without; if room were not left for repentance, and hope given of pardon upon repentance, what would become of us? Let the conversion of sinners, which is the joy of Heaven, be our joy, and never our grief."*[3]

God needs loving, accepting, and compassionate people—not accepting of sin, but accepting God's forgiveness of sin for all who repent.

> *And we have seen and testify that the Father has sent his Son to be the Savior of the world. If anyone acknowledges that Jesus is the Son of God, God lives in them and they in God. And so we know and rely on the love God has for us.*
>
> *God is love. Whoever lives in love lives in God, and God in them. This is how love is made complete among us so that we will have confidence on the day of judgment: In this world we are like Jesus.*
>
> *There is no fear in love. But perfect love drives out fear, because fear has to do with punishment. The one who fears is not made perfect in love.*

---

3. Matthew Henry, *Matthew Henry's Commentary on the Whole Bible: Jonah*, http://www.biblegateway.com/ resources/matthew-henry/Jonah.

> *We love because he first loved us. Whoever claims to love God yet hates a brother or sister is a liar. For whoever does not love their brother and sister, whom they have seen, cannot love God, whom they have not seen. And he has given us this command: Anyone who loves God must also love their brother and sister.*
>
> *1 John 4:14–21*

Having been abused not once but multiple times as a child, I do not like alcoholics, addicts, abusers, or pedophiles. (Who does?) Ironically, I grew up to become an addict: giving me a whole new perspective on things.

Now my heart bleeds for those who are torn apart and held in bondage by addiction. My passions are with those who suffer from addiction. It's easy to follow God when He says, "I want you to minister to children who are broken because of addiction and abuse, and to the addicts who cannot see past where they are right now." My answer is a resounding "Yes, Lord! Here I am; send me."

But what if He asks me to minister to the abuser or the pedophile? What will I say then? Will I try to ignore Him or run away from Him? We cannot let our hurts, fears, and prejudices get in the way of God's calling for our lives.

> *But to you who are listening I say: Love your enemies, do good to those who hate you, bless those who curse you, pray for those who mistreat you.*
>
> *Luke 6:27–28*

CHAPTER TWENTY-SEVEN

MICAH

He has shown you, O mortal, what is good. And what does the Lord require of you? To act justly and to love mercy and to walk humbly with your God.

Micah 6:8

WHAT GOD REQUIRES

(Micah Chapters 1–7)

Micah, a prophet of the Lord, said to the people,
"Listen to the Lord who speaks from His holy temple.
The Sovereign Lord has made accusations against you.
He is coming from his dwelling place to see what you do.

"He treads on the heights of the earth: the mountains melt.
Because of the sins of His people, punishment will be dealt.
Samaria and the temple will become a heap of rubble.
All the way to Jerusalem, this plague has spread trouble.

"A conqueror will come and you will no longer be free.
The people will be exiled and the nobles will flee.
Suffering will come to those who plan iniquity.
Against these people, God has planned calamity."

"God said, *my words are good for those who are upright.
Yet my people rise against me like an enemy ready to fight.
Go away! You have defiled and ruined your resting place.
But in due time, I will lead you out by my grace.*

"Rulers and leaders should embrace justice.
Instead they have lost their moral compass.
You will cry out to God, but He will not hear.
He will hide His face and not draw near."

As for those prophets who lead my people astray,
says the Lord, *you will see night instead of day.
You seers and diviners will be ashamed and disgraced.
You will not find answers, and you will cover your face.*

"In the last days, Mount Zion will be renowned.
People will come to the temple from all around."
In that day, says the Lord, *I will gather the weak.
I will assemble the exiles and those brought to grief.*

"In Babylon, the exiles will be rescued and redeemed.
Out of Bethlehem will come a ruler of all, the king.
His greatness will reach to the ends of the earth.
He will be our Peace from the time of His birth."

My people, what have I done to you? asks the Lord.
*What have I done to make you despise my word?
I delivered you from Egypt and redeemed you from slavery.
I sent you Moses, Aaron, and Gideon, who showed bravery.*

"Remember the righteous acts the Lord has done for you.
For your sins, He does not ask for sacrifice or ado.
He has shown you what is required and what should be sought:
to act justly, to love mercy, and to walk humbly with your God."

CHAPTER TWENTY-EIGHT

NAHUM

The Lord is good, a refuge in times of trouble. He cares for those who trust in him,

Nahum 1:7

NINEVEH AGAIN

(Nahum Chapters 1–3)

Once again God prophesied against the city of Nineveh.
These are the words given to Nahum from God above:
The Lord is slow to anger, but He is great in power.
He will not leave the guilty unpunished in their hour.

His power is displayed in the storm and whirlwind.
The clouds are the dust of His feet beneath Him.
He rebukes the sea and rivers, and they run dry.
The mountains quake, and the hills melt away.

The earth and all who live in it tremble at his presence.
Who can stand against the wrath of the God of Heaven?
The Lord is good, and He is a refuge in times of trouble.
He cares for those who trust in him, who are humble.

But to those who scheme against the Lord,
He will give them their just reward.
But the Lord will restore the splendor of His people,
though destroyers have laid waste and done evil.

The Lord says, *I will expose your sin and shame.*
Those who see you will give you all the blame.
They will not mourn for you nor comfort you.
You will find no healing in anything you do.

CHAPTER TWENTY-NINE

HABAKKUK

Lord, I have heard of your fame; I stand in awe of your deeds, Lord. Repeat them in our day, in our time make them known; in wrath remember mercy.

Habakkuk 3:2

THE LORD'S JUSTICE

(Habakkuk Chapters 1–3)

This is the complaint of the prophet Habakkuk:
Destruction and violence have gone amok.
How long must I call for help when You won't listen?
Instead, Lord, I see injustice, conflict, and division.

The Lord says, *Take notice Habakkuk, and be amazed.
I will do something you will not believe in your days.
I am raising up Babylon to execute judgment on my people,
because they are treacherous and they do nothing but evil.*

I will stand watch and station myself on the ramparts.
I will listen to what God says and answer with my heart.
"Write down my words and take them to the people;"
says the Lord, *the end will soon come to their evil."*

*The proud trust in themselves, and they are wicked,
but the righteous person is faithful and does good.
You will soon suffer the effects of what you have done.
The harm you have caused will be repaid one by one.*

"I am in awe of Your greatness and Your deeds, Lord.
Repeat them again in our day according to Your word.
In Your wrath, please remember Your mercy and grace.
The Heavens and earth are filled with Your glory and praise."

"Your splendor is like the sunrise, and power comes from Your hand.
You look and the nations tremble; the earth shakes when You stand
You came to save Your anointed and to deliver Your people.
You march on forever, and You defeat the powers of evil.

"My heart pounds and my lips quiver at the sound of You.
I will rejoice in the Lord, and wait for Your justice true.
I will be joyful in my Sovereign Lord, God my Savior.
He is my strength and hope, in Him I place my favor."

Sidebar: Habakkuk

WHEN THE WAITING IS THE MESSAGE

> *I will stand at my watch and station myself on the ramparts;
> I will look to see what he will say to me… "For the vision is yet for the appointed time;*
> *It hastens toward the goal and it will not fail. Though it tarries, wait for it; For it will certainly come, it will not delay." (God)*
>
> *Habakkuk 2:1–3*

The process of waiting for a message from God is just as important as the message itself. God promises that He will do whatever He says at just the right time. When we wait for Him, He will not delay. We are willing to wait for things that we feel are important to us (a phone call, a grocery checkout line, etc.).

Yet we refuse to wait on God. Are those other things more important than God? Do we place less value on Him? And what happens when we don't wait and we try to do things on our own? Is that our pride saying we know better than God, or we can do better than God?

Instead of depending on our own resources and power, we should depend on our faith and God's faithfulness. His promises are true. If we trust in Him, we should wait for Him to speak, to move, and to do. We should approach God and His Word with anticipation expecting Him to move.

In the past, when I felt like my prayers were unheard, I felt like I was unimportant to God, like He didn't care about me and I began to doubt that He wanted to speak to me. Like Habakkuk, I desperately need to hear from God, but I have doubted, questioned, and even accused God when I have felt like He wasn't listening or answering. I have asked "How long?" or "Why?" so many times.

When I become discouraged, I fall into a vicious cycle of unbelief. The more I doubt, the less I talk and listen to God. Then the less I talk to God, the more I doubt, and on and on...

But the heroes of faith in the Bible did not walk away despondent when they didn't get the answer they wanted or when they wanted it. They looked expectantly and eagerly for the response that God would offer. Just as God told Habakkuk, even when I cannot see God moving and working, He is always at work—even in the silence.

When I change my level of expectancy, a different type of cycle begins. The more I believe and expect God to move, the more I seek Him and listen for His voice. Then the more I listen, the more I believe.

While trying to buy a house over a five year period, I became so discouraged and desperate that I was willing to settle for any house I thought we could get. But after numerous disappointments, my reaction became completely different because I started trusting God for His will and for good things to happen. Instead of my usual, "Wah Wah, God doesn't love me... Why can't I have it?" ranting, I had peace. Instantly, I knew that God had something better in mind and I trusted Him—and He did!

Two years ago, we bought the house of our dreams.

There are still other personal areas of my life that God is asking me to break the cycle of unbelief, so I must continue to believe and trust in Him, and never stop listening for Him to speak to me. I must stay thankful and trust that He hears and answers me. I must keep letting Him grow my faith and confidence in Him. He truly is a rewarder of those who diligently seek Him. He loves us with unconditional, everlasting love, and He hears us when we call.

CHAPTER THIRTY

ZEPHANIAH

The Lord your God is with you, the Mighty Warrior who saves. He will take great delight in you; in his love he will no longer rebuke you, but will rejoice over you with singing.

Zephaniah 3:17

I THE LORD, HAVE SPOKEN

(Zephaniah Chapters 1–3)

Stand in the presence of the Sovereign Lord.
Be silent before Him and do not say a word.
The awesome day of the Lord's judgment is near.
Those who practice idolatry will weep with tears.

A cry of alarm will sound,
as the punishment of God comes down.
On that day, says the Lord, *cries will echo throughout.*
Wail in sorrow, you who are complacent and who doubt.

That terrible day of the Lord is near.
It comes quickly and with bitter tears.
Your silver and gold will not save you cowards
for the entire land will be devoured.

Gather together, you shameless nation.
Pray for protection from God's agitation.
Gather before God's judgment begins;
before there is no more time to repent.

The remnant of my people will rest at night.
I will restore their prosperity and be kind.
Those who taunt my people will be destroyed—
as completely as Sodom and Gomorrah.

They will receive the wages of their pride,
for they have scoffed at these people of Mine.
I, the Lord of Heaven's armies have spoken,
says the Lord, *my commandments will not be broken.*

What sorrow awaits rebellious, polluted Jerusalem,
the city of violence and crime, so gruesome.
No one can tell them anything; they refuse all correction.
They do not draw near to God or trust in His direction.

Yet the Lord is still with them, and He hands down justice.
He does not fail but purifies His people who are corrupted.
The people who are scattered will come together to worship.
On that day, they will not be ashamed or rebel against His Spirit.

Those people who remain will trust in the Lord and be humble.
They will not tell lies, deceive, or spread trouble.
They will eat and sleep in safety, and no one will make them afraid.
Sing, shout, be glad, rejoice with all your heart, and pray.

For the Lord your mighty Savior is living among you.
He will take delight in you with gladness anew.

ZEPHANIAH

With his love, He will calm all your fears.
With singing, He will dry all your tears.

I will help the helpless, and the weak I will save.
I will bring together those who were chased away.
I will give glory and fame to my people who are broken.
I will restore their fortunes. I, the Lord, have spoken.'"

CHAPTER THIRTY-ONE

HAGGAI

"Be strong, all you people of the land,... and work. For I am with you," declares the Lord Almighty.
Haggai 2:4

REBUILDING GOD'S HOUSE

(Haggai Chapters 1–2)

The word of the Lord came through Haggai the prophet.
To the king and the priest, this is what the Lord says,
It is time for you to stop working so hard when you never have enough.
It is time to build my house so that I may receive honor in Heaven above.

While you are busy with your own houses, Mine lays in disrepair.
Because of this, your wells have been dry and your crops bare.
Then the leaders and the people obeyed the voice of the Lord.
So Haggai, the Lord's messenger, gave the people this word:

THE BIBLE IN POETRY

I am with you, declares the Lord,
The people were stirred up and began to work.
Be strong, declares the Lord, *for I am with you.*
My Spirit goes with you in whatever you do.

I will fill this temple with the glory of the Lord.
It will be greater than the temple that was before.
In this house of God I will give you peace.
From this day on, you will be blessed by me.

CHAPTER THIRTY-TWO

ZECHARIAH

For this is what the Lord Almighty says: "...whoever touches you touches the apple of His eye."

Zechariah 2:8

RETURN TO ME

(Zechariah Chapters 1–14)

The word of the Lord came to the prophet Zechariah:
These are the words of the Lord God Almighty,
Turn back to me, and I will turn back to you.
Turn away from the evil things that you do.

These are the words I said to your ancestors before.
But they would not listen or pay attention to my words.
They repented and said, "The Lord has shown us justice.
He has done to us what we deserve, just as He promised."

During the night, I had a vision of a man on a red horse.
Behind him were red, brown, and white horses—three more.

I asked about the three horses and was told,
"Over all the earth, the Lord has told them to go."

They reported back, "The whole world is at peace and at rest.
An angel asked, "How long, Lord, will you not show mercy to those you love best?"
Then the Lord spoke kind and comforting words to the angel:
"I am angry at the nations that have harmed my people.

"I will return to Jerusalem with mercy and rebuild my sanctuary.
I will comfort them and once again, they will overflow with prosperity."
Then I saw four horns and four craftsmen before me.
The craftsmen removed the horns that had scattered my cities.

Then I saw a man with a measuring line in his hand.
He was going to measure Jerusalem and see where they stand.
Even though Jerusalem has no walls, I will be a wall of fire around it,
declares the Lord God Almighty, *and I will be its glory within.*

Anyone who harms you harms the apple of my eye,
and I will not let them stand nor will I let them slide.
Rejoice and be happy for I am coming, and I will live among you.
Many nations will be joined with me, and Jerusalem will I choose.

Though you are dressed in filthy clothes, I will put fine garments on you.
Walk in obedience to me, and I will take away your sin and make you new.
I am going to bring my servant, Who is the Branch,
and in a day, I will remove the sin of this land.

Then I saw another vision and I asked, "What does this mean?"
The Lord said, "What are you mighty mountain, before me?
It is not by might nor by power but by my Spirit,
The foundation has been laid and the temple will be completed.

"Though you are few and weak, you will finish this temple stone by stone, with shouts of thanksgiving for God's mercy because it was by grace alone."

ZECHARIAH

Then I saw a flying scroll with words on both sides.
"I will send it to those people who cheat and lie.

"I will send it to those who steal," said God Almighty.
"Their houses will be destroyed completely."
Then I saw the iniquity and wickedness of the people,
and the city of Babylon that was full of evil.

I saw four chariots coming out of the mountains.
Then there were different horses, all powerful.
The angel of God told me, "These are the four spirits of Heaven
going out from the Lord's presence."

The one with the black horses went toward the north country,
and the dappled horses went south, before me.
The one with the white horses went toward the west.
As the black horses went north, they gave God's Spirit rest.

Zechariah said, "Again the word of the Lord came to me as before.
It was never for me that you prayed, fasted, and mourned.
All I wanted was for you to show justice, mercy, and compassion to one another.
Do not oppress the widow or the fatherless, the poor or the foreigner.

I will save my people from the countries of the east and the west.
I will bring them back to me, and I will be faithful and righteous.
The seed will grow and the vine will yield its fruit.
The ground will produce crops and the Heaven's dew.

All these things will be an inheritance to the remnant.
I will save them, and they will be a blessing again.
Do not be afraid, but do these things instead.
Let your judgement be true, the Lord God says.

Rejoice greatly and shout, and love truth and peace.
Your king comes to you, righteous and victorious, see!
He comes lowly, riding on a colt, on the foal of a donkey.
He will bring peace to the nations; the battle bow will be broken.

His rule will extend to the ends of the earth, from sea to sea.
Because of my blood covenant, I will set you prisoners free.
I will restore you, and you will no longer be without hope.
I will shield you, and your well-being I will promote.

I will send thunderstorms in the springtime when you ask for rain.
I will be with you when you fight, and the enemy will be put to shame.
I will restore you because of my compassion when you turn to me.
Your hearts will rejoice in me, and you will be secure and redeemed.

I will make Jerusalem an immovable rock for all nations.
All who try to move it will hurt themselves because of the strong foundation.
I will keep a watchful eye over Judah, and their people will comment,
"These people are strong because the Lord is God of Jerusalem."

The Lord of Heaven and earth who created everything declares,
On that day, anyone who attacks Jerusalem will be destroyed and will despair.
I will pour out my Spirit of grace and prayer on my beloved people.
They will look on the One they have pierced and mourn for their evil.

On that day, a fountain will be opened to my people by me
to purify them from their sin and cleanse them from their impurity.
I will refine them like silver and test them like gold. "The Lord is our God,"
they will say.
I will say, These are my people, *and I will answer them when they call on*
my name.

CHAPTER THIRTY-THREE

MALACHI

But who can endure the day of his coming? Who can stand when he appears? For he will be like a refiner's fire or a launderer's soap.

Malachi 3:2

DISHONORING THE LORD

(Malachi Chapters 1–4)

These are the words of the prophet Malachi to the people:
God says, *I have loved my people deeply even when they did evil.*
"How have you loved us, Lord?" the people responded.
God answers, *I loved Jacob, and I brought you out of bondage.*

You dishonor me with your polluted sacrifices that are worthless. You bring things that are defiled instead of bringing me your best. Why do you sin against me by defiling the altar and testing my patience? For I am a great king and my name is to be feared among the nations.

There will be consequences if you don't listen and obey.
I am sending you this warning so that my covenant will stay.
The priest Levi kept this covenant of life and of peace.
He revered my name, spoke truth, and walked upright before me.

But your priests have turned from the way and have caused many to stumble.
You have violated my covenant and will be despised and humbled.
You flood my altar with weeping, wailing, and tears
because I no longer look with favor on you here.

I will send my messenger who will prepare the way before me.
Then the Lord you are seeking will come, and you will see.
I will refine you like gold and silver in the fire.
You will be righteous and do what is required.

You oppress widows and orphans and rob the Lord
because you do not bring the entire tithe into the store.
There should be food in my house for the sick, the needy, and the poor.
Test me, and watch blessings flood out as I open Heaven's doors.

You say "serving the Lord is futile—what do we gain?"
But there is a scroll of remembrance for those who honor my name.
When I act, they will be my treasured possession and I will spare them.
Then you will see the difference between the righteous and those who sin.

www.ingramcontent.com/pod-product-compliance
Lightning Source LLC
Chambersburg PA
CBHW062102080426
42734CB00012B/2722